HIDDEN HISTORY

of

LAKE WINNIPESAUKEE

HIDDEN HISTORY

HISTORY

of

LAKE WINNIPESAUKEE

Glenn A. Knoblock

THE
History PRESS

Published by The History Press
Charleston, SC
www.historypress.com

Copyright © 2021 by Glenn A. Knoblock
All rights reserved

Front cover: Approaching Lake Station, Wolfeboro, 1906. *Courtesy of the Library of Congress*.

First published 2021

Manufactured in the United States

ISBN 9781467148467

Library of Congress Control Number: 2021931130

For my grandson Gordon, a future explorer in New Hampshire who is just getting started. I look forward to sharing many adventures with you!

CONTENTS

ACKNOWLEDGEMENTS

First and foremost, I'd like to thank Terry, my wife and constant companion for the last forty years, for her help and support in this book endeavor. She has been with me every step of the way as we journeyed all the way around Lake Winnipesaukee some ten times during the course of on-site research and picture-taking activities. Having her by my side as an enthusiastic supporter has made this work, by far, the most enjoyable of all the books I've written over the years.

For research help with the book, thanks go to John Dickey of the Gilmanton Historical Society; Lauren Hansen, museum and collector coordinator of the Sandwich Historical Society; and Marty Cornelissen of the Alton Historical Society for providing research materials or clarifying points of information. Thanks, too, are due to Mike Young and Fred Merrill of the New Hampshire Veterans Association. Fred met with me twice, once in company with Mike, at their historic encampment site at the Weirs and offered not only a full tour of the site but also a number of old photographs of the site. Mike, who served his organization as longtime quartermaster, offered his great knowledge on the site while touring inside some of the regimental buildings and shared information as to how the site has evolved and how it has been maintained over the years. He could write his own full-length book treatment on the site if he were so inclined, and I hope he does. A prolific poet, Mike also shared several of his compositions, including one about the site in question, which were quite thought-provoking. In Ossipee, I wish to thank Lois Bennett Sweeney of the Historical Society of Ossipee for sharing her personal reminiscences of the Wilkins family and their personal photos and records, likely one of the few, if not the only, collection of materials relating to a Black family in northern New Hampshire from the early twentieth century. Thanks, too, go to Cal Elliot of Ossipee, who warmly opened his home—once the home of Cary Wilkins—to me and shared his insights on the property and the construction details of the house. Without a doubt, this home is in good hands for the foreseeable future—a real historic gem. In Alton, great thanks go to Paul La Rochelle for allowing me to conduct an extensive interview about the ice runway he has come to operate. His dedication to his community is readily apparent, and it's no wonder he was honored by the local Masonic chapter for his efforts in 2018. Thanks, too, go to veteran commercial pilot Rand Peck of Amherst, New Hampshire, whom I met in that town during an unrelated historical event, only to find out that he was a pilot who knew Alton well and kindly agreed to provide the photos for that chapter. To see more of Rand's aviation photographs and learn more about his excellent career, please visit his online site at www.randpeckaviationphotography.com.

My apologies in advance to anyone I may have left out inadvertently, and as all historians must state, any errors that have crept into this book are entirely my own. Finally, I'd like to thank Mike Kinsella, acquisitions editor for The History Press/Arcadia Publishing. He has been excellent to work with, and it was at his suggestion that this book was written. I'm glad I took up his suggestion and turned it into reality.

All photographs and illustrations are by the author or from my collection unless otherwise noted.

—Glenn Knoblock
Wolfeboro Falls, New Hampshire
November 2020

INTRODUCTION

The Lake Winnipesaukee area of New Hampshire has long been renowned for its nature setting and natural aquatic beauty, and since the 1850s, it has been a place where thousands of people have come annually to rest, relax and spend time away from their otherwise busy lives back at home. While the area is "lake life" focused today, few people, including even local residents, realize that the area surrounding the "big lake," the largest in New Hampshire and the second largest located entirely in New England, also has a wide-ranging history that dates far back in time. Indeed, before the white man first came to Lake Winnipesaukee's shores, Native Americans were the first to spend their summers here, having done so for thousands of years before America was colonized by Europeans. While colonial-era explorers, adventurers and merchants from New Hampshire and Massachusetts traversed the region from the 1650s onward, it would not be until the era of the French and Indian Wars of the 1750s and 1760s that permanent settlements were first established. From that time to the present, the towns surrounding Lake Winnipesaukee have developed their own unique history, and there are many interesting aspects of that history that deserve a wider audience. At first glance, the area does not belie that history to the casual observer; there are plenty of well-known places to hike, swim and enjoy all that the lake has to offer. But the places where history happened, sites that might attract the eye of the local and the vacationer alike, are lacking. Or are they? In fact, the area does have its interesting historical sites, but they are largely hidden, sometimes in plain sight. No, George Washington never slept anywhere in the area, nor are there any famous battlefields and but few surviving colonial-era dwellings, but nonetheless, each town has something to share, and collectively viewed and understood, the history that they embody gives one a more complete view of the Lake Winnipesaukee area. That's what this book is mostly about, and so, whether you reside in the area as I do, have been a seasonal resident or tourist for years or even if this is your first visit to the area, it is my hope that the historical vignettes here presented will offer further opportunities for local exploration, as well as enhance your appreciation of an area you have already come to love.

All of the accounts you will read about are true and really did happen here in the towns represented, which are New Durham, Alton, Gilford, Gilmanton, Laconia, Meredith, Center Harbor, Sandwich, Moultonborough, Tuftonboro, Ossipee and Wolfeboro. I have presented the facts here as known, and where supposition rather than fact is presented, it is so noted. In most cases, I have presented the historical sites where these events took place, although in several instances there is no tangible place to visit and experience, so the reader will have to use their imagination. One thing that the reader will note are the common threads that run through this work. Though all are tied to Lake Winnipesaukee by proximity, they are also tied together by broader events like the Civil War and the coming of the railroad, sometimes in unusual ways that are not commonly known, thus the term "hidden" in the book title. Each of the chapters in this book, which are loosely arranged chronologically, can be read separately and at random if so desired, but these common threads are easily discernible. Too, though the book discusses many physical sites, this book is just as much about people as it is about buildings, boats or the lake—and not just the famous and wealthy, but also the lesser known and the downtrodden. Those whose lives were hard seldom get their due in the history books. However, I have tried to avoid that mistake in this book, and though their stories can often be uncomfortable, they are nonetheless interesting and need to be told to give a more complete account of what life around Lake Winnipesaukee really was like. Of some of the events in this book we know a lot, while of several but little is known. In some cases, a full story can be presented, but in others, especially for sites like the Laconia State School, space limits permit but a general account, and the reader will have to go to other sources to get full and exacting details, some of which I have listed at the end of this book. Indeed, for those who are historically minded, I hope this book serves as an inspiration and springboard to seek out further historical information, whether it be in published town histories and the like or exploring what your local historical society has to offer. No matter how this book serves you, the one thing I know for certain is this: after a full reading, you will look at the area around Lake Winnipesaukee as more than just a place to "get away from it all."

Chapter 1

Massachusetts Stakes Its Claim

The state of New Hampshire has long had a contentious relationship with its neighbor to the south. Workers who live in New Hampshire but work in Massachusetts appreciate the well-paying job opportunities but have long disdained paying the Commonwealth's income tax and have long referred to that state as "Taxachusetts." Likewise, New Hampshire residents love it when Massachusetts tourists visit the state to spend their hard-earned leisure dollars, but after a while, they are quite anxious to have them return from whence they came. Indeed, even though New Hampshire has a symbiotic relationship with Massachusetts, the two states have a hard time getting along. So, what's the deal? What is the basis for this fraught relationship? The answer to that question, perhaps, lies hidden in plain sight at the Weirs in Laconia. It is there that you will find the Endicott Rock State Park–Historic Site, located right alongside the Weirs Channel, which connects Paugus Bay with Lake Winnipesaukee. In this park is the historic Endicott Rock, which dates back to 1652. It is here where the complicated relationship between New Hampshire and Massachusetts—dating back nearly four hundred years to the early colonial days—was marked in stone. Most New Hampshire folks I talk to, and many visitors as well, visit this park for its beach, but relatively few pay much attention to Endicott Rock, or if they do know of its existence, they think of it as another version of Plymouth Rock. The rock itself is about five feet long by four feet in width and has carved in the center, in old-fashioned script (where a capital *J* resembles a capital *I*), "WP" (for "Worshipful"), followed by "Iohn

Endicot Gov," surrounded by four sets of initials of the men who discovered the rock on August 1, 1652. From top to bottom, left to right, these are "EI" (Edward Johnson), "SW" (Simon Willard), "IS" (John Sherman) and "II" (Jonathan Ince). Since 1892, the rock been housed in a granite structure, which is roofed but has open sides, which permit a view of the rock. And since 1901, it has had several versions of a statue of an Indian mounted on top; more about him later on. So, what is the significance of this rock? Well, it has to do with settling the New Hampshire–Massachusetts boundary line, which has been one of the most disputed in our nation's history.

The genesis of this conflict began in 1622, when Captain John Mason received from the King of England a grant of land that would form the basis of the New Hampshire colony, which was first permanently settled the following year. Just six years later, in 1629, land to the south was granted to the Puritans when the Massachusetts Bay Colony received its charter from King Charles I. These two colonies might have coexisted peacefully, except for the fact that they were managed quite differently. The Puritans set out in a great fleet of ships in 1630 to establish their colony in the area that became Boston and there set up a colonial government. In New Hampshire, however, things proceeded quite differently, as Mason himself never came to New Hampshire. Though he did send settlers, no formal colonial government was set up in his new lands, and he was instead running affairs from afar in England. This worked until December 1635, when Mason died suddenly, leaving his financial affairs, including ownership of his New Hampshire lands, in limbo and the colony without an established government. The several towns of the colony governed their own matters for several years, but it soon became apparent that a better system was needed, especially in regard to mutual matters regarding religion, as well as military affairs during times of conflicts with the Indians. It was for this reason that the towns in New Hampshire sought the protection of neighboring Massachusetts and, in 1641, formally joined with that colony. Indeed, New Hampshire would be governed by Massachusetts from 1641 to 1675, and it would not be until 1680 that New Hampshire finally separated and formed its own colonial government. This union between the two colonies was always uneasy, and as New Hampshire grew and prospered, the idea of becoming independent was always in the background.

Meanwhile, the thriving Massachusetts Bay Colony was growing in power and was anxious to expand its territory and saw an opportunity to acquire both New Hampshire and Maine land as its own. Now, the Massachusetts charter used the Merrimack River as its guide. All land between that river—

which it was assumed flowed on its course entirely westward toward the Pacific Ocean—and the Charles River to the south was granted to the Puritans. However, as the Massachusetts colony grew in size and lands to the west were explored, it soon became clear that the Merrimack River did not flow west but turned north around the area of Dracut (which was established in 1653) and continued in that direction for an unknown distance. While Massachusetts authorities did not know how far north the Merrimack's course ran, they did see an opportunity to claim all the land to the east, which included all of settled New Hampshire and Maine at the time. Indeed, if they could establish where the headwaters of the Merrimack were located, by right of their charter, in their opinion, all that land and the towns within would be theirs to govern.

To that end, an expedition was formed in 1652 to determine the headwaters of the Merrimack. Its leader was Captain Edward Johnson of Woburn, later distinguished as the author of *The Wonderworking Providence of Sion's Savior in New England* (1654), an early history of the Massachusetts Bay Colony that was widely read. He was accompanied by Captain Simon Willard, an explorer and trader who had many dealings with the Natives in northern Massachusetts; Sergeant John Sherman, a surveyor; and Harvard student Jonathan Ince, who acted as a surveyor and was able to speak the Native language proficiently. The group was accompanied by two Indian guides, Potanhum and Ponbakin, who knew the river well, and they began to make their way northward in July. The journey proceeded with no major incidents and reached the head of the Merrimack at the modern-day town of Franklin, at the confluence of the Pemigewasset and Winnipesaukee Rivers. It is interesting that the expedition subsequently chose to follow the waters of the Winnipesaukee River northeast rather than the course of the Pemigewasset River, which would have taken them another forty miles northward to present-day Franconia, allowing Massachusetts to claim even more land. Though uncertain, it was perhaps the Indian guides who persuaded Johnson as to his course, taking them another eleven miles up the river to Lake Winnipesaukee, via Lake Winnisquam and Opechee Bay, rather than deeper into their Native territory. Here, at the river's entry into Lake Winnipesaukee, the Massachusetts men saw the ancient Indian village of Aquedoctan, which was then uninhabited. This village was a summering place where Native peoples had come to fish for thousands of years before Europeans arrived in New Hampshire, the Massachusetts men being the first to come to this part of New Hampshire. It was here, at a determined latitude, that the Endicott Rock, named after the Massachusetts colonial governor, was found and inscribed by Jonathan Ince and used as a marker to denote, three miles north of this spot, the northern border of Massachusetts.

Once the expedition returned homeward, Ince and Sherman reported their findings to a colonial council, and then what happened? Nothing! The rock lay as it had for years, among the weirs, the stone fishing traps of the Indians. The area would not even see permanent settlement until the 1760s, over one hundred years later, and even then, the rock and its border-marking purpose was ignored. In fact, the border between New Hampshire and Massachusetts was finally settled in 1740. The royal commissioners who finally determined the matter distinctly pointed out that the country had been unexplored when the original grant to Massachusetts was made, and it was determined to be inequitable to base the border on the northward course of the Merrimack. Thus, the matter was settled once and for all and the present border between the two future states established. Interestingly, the tactics that Massachusetts used to claim New Hampshire territory were also applied to the settlements north of New Hampshire in Maine. While New Hampshire never accepted the Endicott Rock boundary, the isolated colonists in Maine did, with the result that from that time until 1820, when Maine became a state, their land was part of and governed by Massachusetts.

As for Endicott Rock itself, it has remained in its original location since settlers have arrived here, neither displaced nor defaced, but also not celebrated in any way. It remained visible until the early 1800s, when it became submerged after a dam was built in the area and raised the level of the lake. It was rediscovered in 1832 when water in the Weirs was drained when a channel was dug to allow passage for the steamship *Belknap* from the lake to Laconia. From that point onward, it seems to have been regarded more as a curiosity than a historic site. However, efforts to preserve the rock eventually prevailed, with it finally being enclosed in its present structure in 1892. Interestingly, the landscape around Endicott Rock has changed greatly over the years. It originally sat in the Weirs Channel, with entry to the site enabled by a man-made causeway. However, over the years, that land has been filled in so that it now sits on a small peninsula. Though the land for Endicott Park was donated to the Town of Laconia in 1953, the small peninsula with Endicott Rock, less than a half acre in size, is still owned by the state.

One other distinctive feature of the Endicott Rock site is the Indian sculpture that is found on top of the enclosure. The original statue was made of zinc and was placed there in 1901, procured from a New York company

Endicott Rock, Weirs, N. H.

Above: A postcard view of Endicott Rock enclosure from the 1930s, before the area around it was filled in, and the causeway that allowed for access.

Right: The Endicott Rock granite enclosure as it looks today.

The original Native American statue that adorned the top of the Endicott Rock enclosure, now on display in the Laconia Public Library.

that sold cigar store advertising items. The Indian sculpture was named after Captain Jack, a symbol of the Captain Jack Tobacco Company. Known as Kintpuash in his Native tongue, Captain Jack had no connection to New Hampshire whatsoever, being a chief of the Modoc tribe in California and Oregon. He was in the news for resisting the U.S. government's efforts to displace his people in the brief Modoc War and killed two peace commissioners in 1873. He was subsequently captured and executed for what were called "war crimes," the only Native American leader to be so charged and executed by the American government. This statue remained in place at Endicott Rock until about 1983, when it was removed after suffering a lightning strike and vandalism. The statue now resides in a balcony above the reading room of the Gale Memorial Library (the Laconia Public Library) in Laconia. It was replaced in 2005 with the current sculpture executed by Robert Morton, whose work is an historically accurate representation of the Native Americans of the Lake Winnipesaukee region and distinguished by its animal headdress.

So, there you have it—a colonial artifact placed by a rival colony trying to stake its claim (or steal it, depending on your perspective) on New Hampshire land and tangible evidence of the first white men to visit the southern shore of Lake Winnipesaukee over 368 years ago.

CHAPTER 2

THE TRUE STORY OF AMERICA'S OLDEST SUMMER RESORT

B eautifully situated on the shores of Lake Winnipesaukee, at the head of a large bay that bears its name, Wolfeboro, incorporated in 1770, is the second-oldest town situated on the lake and one of the most important. As you come into town, you may notice the signs that proclaim it to be "America's Oldest Summer Resort," and as you approach the center of town and get a full view of Lake Winnipesaukee, whether for the first time or the hundredth, you can understand why it's so popular. You might even wonder at what location on the lake this first resort was located, but if you're looking for some kind of plaque or historical marker, your search will be in vain for the simple fact that you're on the wrong lake. That's right! While the first resort home was indeed built in Wolfeboro, beginning way back in 1768, it was *not* on Lake Winnipesaukee but on Lake Wentworth to the northeast. In fact, modern-day Wolfeboro, first known as Smith's Bridge Village, would not gain the resort status that it has today until many decades later. Now, to be fair, Lake Wentworth, the state's seventh-largest lake and first known as Smith's Pond, is connected to the big lake by the Smith River and Crescent Lake, and in the 1700s, it was often referred to as "Winnipesiokee Pond." Of course, the question for us in the modern day is where was this first resort and who was its owner? The site of the very first resort home on the lake is found in the Governor Wentworth Historic Site State Park, located on the shores of Lake Wentworth at 56 Wentworth Farm Road, off State Route 109. This site does have a sign on the highway, but its entranceway, a dirt road, is not clearly marked. Perhaps because of this, it is one of the least visited of New Hampshire's state historic sites and has even been deemed by some one of the least interesting. This site is truly a case of the more you know beforehand, the more you can appreciate what the site represents.

The owner of this first summer home was New Hampshire's last royal governor, John Wentworth (1737–1820), of the prominent Wentworth family dynasty. John Wentworth was the son of the province's lieutenant governor and the nephew of Governor Benning Wentworth, whom he succeeded in 1767. Though servants to the Crown and the seat of royal authority, the Wentworth family governors were born and bred in New Hampshire, perhaps the most distinguished family in the colony. When Wolfeboro was granted in 1759, most of the early grantees were Portsmouth men, the seat of colonial government, so it's not surprising that the newly appointed governor would take an interest in Wolfeboro. In fact, Wentworth attained four tracts of land along the lake that would come to bear his name when the original grantees failed to live up to their obligations and would later purchase several adjacent lots, thereby owning over 3,500 acres of land, along with 1,500 additional acres abutting in neighboring Brookfield and New Durham. With this land, Wentworth hoped to establish a landed estate, one that perhaps was inspired by the old Wentworth ancestral estate in Yorkshire, England, which he had visited as a young man during his time in England from 1763 to 1767. Though it is clear that Wentworth wanted to establish a country estate, a place where he could get away from the hustle and bustle of Portsmouth, he also hoped to inspire others to develop other newly settled areas in the colony.

In the spring of 1768, Wentworth first began clearing the land of his future estate, the efforts led by his personal overseer, as well as a local hired farmer. Over the next two years, the Wentworth mansion and outbuildings—including a large barn measuring 100 feet long (still standing in 1901) and a caretaker's house—were built, orchards and gardens were planted, a well was dug (still in existence) and stone fences were constructed. Lumber for the house was cut on site, while the bricks were manufactured at a site on Wolfeboro Falls from clay that came from Alton. A hunting park on the estate was also established, delineated by a moat covered with large tree branches, in which were stocked deer and moose for the governor to hunt. The house, whose cellar hole is all that remains today, was 140 feet long and 40 feet wide, of two stories, with a gambrel roof. Inside were at least three fireplaces of white, black and gray marble, with the upstairs East India Room decorated with fine wallpaper depicting scenes of the Orient. One

Artist's conception of the Wentworth summer mansion in Wolfeboro, from Benjamin Parker's *History of the Town of Wolfeborough.*

interior end of the house, probably meant to serve as office or court spaces in the summer months, was never finished.

Finally, in the summer of 1770, the estate was fit for habitation, and Wentworth, with his beautiful wife, Frances Deering Wentworth, along with their many servants and several slaves, visited for the first summer. It is interesting to note that while the family traveled by horse and carriage down the path later called Governor's Road (Route 109), stopping at many inns along the way, the family's household goods arrived by boat from Merrymeeting River in New Durham to Lake Winnipesaukee and subsequently via the Smith River (after being portaged at what today is known as Wolfeboro Falls) and Crescent Lake to Lake Wentworth. Clearly, John Wentworth loved his time in Wolfeboro, taking great interest in hunting, fishing, gardening, planting and continuing the development of his estate. His wife, on the other hand, was less enamored of the country life. She lamented in a 1770 letter to a friend, "I am all alone. The Governor is so busy in directions to his workmen that I am most turned hermit....So now I read or play as I have a mind to do. I get very little of my Governor's company....I don't see him an hour in the day." In this same letter, Frances also clearly shows that she is not the outdoor type, commenting that "elegance is not to be found in the country" and complaining of "tedious walks which the charms of the meadows scarcely make up," on one of which she "lost both my shoes and came home barefoot." That must have given her servants, if not the governor himself, a bit of a laugh. She later comments, "Although I live in the woods, I am fond of knowing what passes in the world," and "nor have my ideas sunk in rural tranquility half enough to prefer a grove to a ball-room." Had she been a visitor in modern times, it seems likely that her cellphone would have remained close at hand. Whether Lady Wentworth ever came to love her time in Wolfeboro is unknown, but doubtful. However, not all of her time here was unpleasant. There was a tree-lined mall that led from the house down to the lake, and just one hundred yards offshore was Turtle Island. A small causeway built to the island allowed her to picnic there with visiting friends.

Governor Wentworth continued to summer in Wolfeboro, making his last visit in the spring of 1775. However, his visit was cut short when news of the Battle at Lexington and Concord came to him in April, and he left in a hurry, taking back with him his personal plate and his favorite horse. He probably thought he would return, but the events of the American

Portraits of Royal Governor John Wentworth and his wife, Frances Deering Wentworth, from Benjamin Parker's *History of the Town of Wolfeborough*.

Revolution in 1775 moved quickly. He and his family fled from Portsmouth to Boston aboard a British warship in June 1775, and the following year, they left there for Nova Scotia.

In fact, Wentworth was a great promoter of the colony and was known for his road building, including the College Road that led to Dartmouth College in the west, which he also played a part in establishing. While Wentworth played a large part in improving and building roads to Wolfeboro, it is also thought that he envisioned a canal being built that connected the big lake to Dover. Governor John Wentworth, in many ways, was a man caught in the times. A native of New Hampshire, he respected the people he governed and sought to improve the colony. When the Crown in the 1760s began passing oppressive tax measures on their colonies, Wentworth may have even played a part in getting the onerous Stamp Act repealed.

After the departure of Wentworth from Wolfeboro, left behind was the slave family that had served them for a brief time (see chapter 13), but the house remained vacant for about seven years. In the meantime, its contents were gathered up. Mark Wentworth, the governor's father, was allowed to retrieve the family furniture and pictures, while other contents were put up for auction. For those locals who were employed by Wentworth on his estate and were owed wages, they received nothing, the new State of New Hampshire voiding all claims against the estate. Finally, in 1782, the mansion and land were sold to the Cabot brothers of Beverly, Massachusetts, but they never became permanent residents, and when the last brother died in 1794, the estate was sold to a series of owners. In 1805, Daniel Raynard of Boston became the last owner of the house, his widow residing there when the mansion burned down in 1820. It was that same year that John Wentworth, then the first baronet of Nova Scotia, died, having never returned to New Hampshire.

Over time, much of the Wentworth land was parceled out and sold, and by 1901, what was left of the estate, according to Wolfeboro historian Benjamin Franklin Parker, consisted of little more than a cellar hole filled with trash, "dilapidated" stone fences, "scraggy apple trees" and "unkempt pasture." Parker commented in his *History of the Town of Wolfeborough New Hampshire*, from which most of the details of this account have been gathered, that, regarding the area of Wentworth's former estate, "the time is coming when it's environs will be appreciated; when the shores and islands of Lake Wentworth will be dotted with cottages; when a road will be constructed, uniting existing highways." If you continue driving past the Governor Wentworth Historic Site and around the lake, you will see that Parker's ideals have come true, albeit to a lesser extent than that along the shores of Lake Winnipesaukee.

The state would eventually acquire a small parcel of the land on which the cellar hole is located, it being donated in 1933 by author and Governor Wentworth biographer Lawrence Shaw Mayo, who had acquired the land in 1925. It has been the hope for over two decades now that a museum might be built here and the park further developed, but the land leading down to the lake is now overgrown with trees, the former mall long gone. While trails on the site were once envisioned, they have yet to be developed, and it is unlikely they ever will be. Of artifacts from the site, some were found during archaeological digs conducted in the mid-1980s, including creamware, pearlware, redware, white salt-glazed stoneware, a few coins and pewter spoons, as well as some iron hinges and a large quantity of nails and other architectural debris. Despite the sparse remainders on the Wentworth site, the cellar hole is impressive, and armed with context, it's not hard to imagine the house that once stood here. In your mind's eye, perhaps you can envision the governor, musket in hand, hunting in his estate park, while Lady Wentworth, equipped with a parasol and with an attendant close at hand, returns from a walk in the meadows, this time still wearing her shoes. A good day, indeed, to be at the lake house.

CHAPTER 3

THE DAWN OF A NEW RELIGION

As you enter the Lakes Region from the southeast, you may be making your way on State Route 11, the main road from Rochester. Several miles from Alton, you will pass through the town of New Durham. It's an old town, incorporated in 1762, and a small one, with a population of about 2,600. As a matter of fact, if you're not paying attention, you might just pass through New Durham without even knowing it. However, it's a town worth exploring, both for its natural beauty as well as its history, and in many ways, it can be seen as the historic religious capital of the Lake Winnipesaukee region and beyond for many miles. This may be surprising, but it's true, for it was here that a former seaman established his own religion, that of the Free Will Baptists, subsequently spreading his doctrine throughout the area and beyond. Today, the denomination has nearly 200,000 members in over 2,300 churches spread out all across the United States. The historic ancestral church of the Free Will Baptists can be seen today at 56 Ridge Road South in New Durham and is one of the most beautifully situated churches in the state, the area of Ridge Road offering a fine view of the surrounding Lakes Region.

The founder of the Free Will Baptist movement was Benjamin Randall (1749–1808), a native of New Castle, New Hampshire. The son of a mariner, he worked as a sailor while young and then learned the trade of a sailmaker, working in the seaport cities of Portsmouth and later Salem and Marblehead in Massachusetts before returning to New Hampshire. Said to have been a pious youth, his religious sensitivities were reawakened in 1770 when he heard the religious sermons of the English evangelist Reverend George Whitefield during his final visit to Portsmouth. Randall would subsequently become an evangelist himself and soon held his own religious meetings. Though nominally a member of the Congregational Church, Randall believed it important that laymen could take part in religious sermons and was soon a thorn in the side of his local minister. Randall was married to Joanna Oram of Kittery, Maine, whose father was also a mariner, in 1771. During the American Revolution, Randall would serve as a soldier in both Massachusetts and Portsmouth-area militia units and even served as an unofficial unit chaplain, with the approval of his commanding officer.

In 1776, Randall began to identify with the Calvinistic Baptist faith and served as a lay preacher, holding revival meetings. However, his animated meetings alienated many in the area, and Randall began to receive personal insults and abuses for his preaching. In 1777, Randall began to travel farther afield to preach, and the following year, he decided to move his family to New Durham. This town had recently dismissed its Congregational minister, so Randall was the only preacher in town and gave periodic sermons at the town meetinghouse (which is still extant), as well as continuing his itinerant preaching in surrounding towns, with New Durham as his base. Unlike most town ministers, who were financially supported by town residents by mandate, Randall only accepted voluntary donations. In 1780, Randall formalized his beliefs and separated from the Calvinistic Baptists, who believed in the concept of predestination, whereby the destination of an individual's soul after death, whether it be Heaven or Hell, was preordained and could not be altered by one's so-called good works during their lifetime. In stark contrast, Randall offered greater hope to his followers, believing that "free salvation" was available to all, but only if they were true believers and repented of their sins. The basis of his beliefs was that individuals had the "free will" to act as they pleased and that God would forgive them for any actions resulting from their free will. Randall was officially ordained as a minister in April 1780, and in June, he drew up Articles of Faith and a Church Covenant in New Durham, and thus the Free Will Baptist Church was born, though the term "Free Will" was not part of the church name until after 1800. From 1780 until his death from tuberculosis in 1808, Elder Benjamin Randall and his disciple preachers would go on to establish over thirty Free Will Baptist church congregations throughout New Hampshire, including in towns as far away as Lebanon and Unity, as well as in many Lakes Region towns, including Wolfeboro, Ossipee, Strafford and Alton.

The First Free Will Baptist Church, New Durham, New Hampshire, built in 1818.

The church on Ridge Road is a simple Greek Revival and Italianate-style structure and was built in 1818–19. Prior to this, church services were held in the old town meetinghouse for a time but mostly in members' homes. The church originally had no tower, its simple lines characteristic of many Lakes Region churches. The bell tower was added in 1869. Today, regular church services are held at the modern First Free Will Baptist Church on Depot Street, but the historic church on Ridge Road, added to the National Register of Historic Places in 1980, is well maintained and is used intermittently when special services are held. It is considered the mother church of the Free Will Baptists, and members come from all over the country to visit this historic site, as well as to visit the burial site of the founder of the church and his family, which is located in a private cemetery just down the road off a poorly maintained dirt road. Indeed, the old mother church in Durham, located in this quietest of settings, is proof yet again that history that affects hundreds of thousands of people often originates in the smallest of places.

CHAPTER 4

SCHOOLMASTER AND WEATHER
FORECASTER EXTRAORDINAIRE

Two sites can be found in Meredith that are related to one of the area's, and New England's, greatest scholars and publishers, Dudley Leavitt. The first and most easily found is the New Hampshire State Historical Marker, erected in 1962, located on Route 25, close to the Meredith–Center Harbor town line and adjacent to the Meredith welcoming sign. The other is the Leavitt Family Cemetery, located on the old Leavitt farm property, less than a mile from the shores of Lake Winnipesaukee, at the end of Quarry Road within the Page Pond and Forest conservation land. A small hike is required to reach this site, but it is not a hard one by any means and well worth the effort. For effect, if you have a copy of an old almanac, you might want to bring that along with you. Walking these lands, you are traversing in the footsteps of one of Meredith's greatest citizens and, in his day, the most famous.

Dudley Leavitt was born in Exeter, New Hampshire, in 1772 and in 1790 graduated from that town's fledgling (now prestigious) Phillips Exeter Academy, which had been established in 1781. The studious Leavitt, from old New England stock and a descendant of Massachusetts colonial governor Thomas Dudley, became a schoolteacher and moved by 1794 to Gilmanton in the Lakes Region, where he married his wife, Judith Glidden. Not only did he continue his studies in Latin and Greek under Reverend Isaac Smith, but he also was employed as the town schoolmaster. While here, Leavitt would serve as a selectman, but he was less interested in town politics and more interested in the written word. His

The New Hampshire State Historical Marker for Dudley Leavitt, sited along Route 25 near the Meredith–Center Harbor town line.

most notable publication was *Leavitt's Farmer's Almanack*, whose first issue came out in 1797, but he also published a town newspaper, the *Gilmanton Gazette*, beginning in 1800 for a few years, as well as the *Farmer's Weekly Magazine* and the *New Hampshire Register* from 1811 to 1817. These last three publications were short-lived, but his almanac soon became a hit and, until the advent of the *Old Farmer's Almanac*, published in Dublin, New Hampshire, beginning in 1939 (founded in Boston in 1792), remained the state's best-known almanac and popular publication, as well as one of New England's. Now, for those who are younger than, say, the age of fifty, you may have but scant knowledge of an almanac and its purpose. Long before the days of cellphones and the Internet, as well as any modern media like television and radio, if you wanted to know simple yet vital (especially to farmers) information—such as the time when the sun would rise or set on any day of the year, what to expect from the weather, on what days the phases of the moon would occur or tidal information—the almanac was your guide. In addition, these small publications, about fifty pages or fewer in length in most cases, often included folksy articles on history or society;

helpful hints for farming, gardening, hunting or food preparation; and useful data about current postage rates, interest rates for banks and state and federal government information. In short, almanacs were a source of both useful information as well as entertainment and something that families liked to keep close at hand, which accounts for the small string loop at the top of each almanac, which allowed for it be hung from a nail in the barn or kitchen, available for quick reference, rather than just sitting on a bookshelf or parlor table.

Dudley Leavitt compiled the astronomical calculations and other data and articles for his almanac for sixty years, from 1797 until six years after his death in 1851. That's right; prior to his death he had already made the necessary calculations for the next six years of his almanac data through the year 1857. Leavitt, indeed, was no slouch when it came to making his publisher's deadline and was just about as exacting and punctual an individual as you might ever find. Perhaps one of the reasons for doing so were his other extensive activities. He continued his noted teaching career for most of the rest of his life, teaching into his seventies, and with the formation of his Meredith Academick School in 1819, just two years after his move to town, he became renowned throughout New Hampshire for his abilities, teaching a wide variety of subjects at a monetary rate that varied based on the type of classes and degree of difficulty. This he did for twenty-seven straight years until his retirement in 1846. He would also author six textbooks, including three on mathematics and two on astronomy, both subjects said to be "his meat and drink," as well as a teacher's and student's daily assistant guide. At his sudden death in 1851, he had two other books complete and ready for publication, one a guide for the academic and practical astronomer and the other a singer's grammar book for both students and performers. He was, truly, a gifted educator. As to his manner, he most certainly had an acerbic wit typical of many New Englanders and did not tolerate any shenanigans in his class. While it is said that he was probably better suited to teach tough young men rather than children, the "Academic Awards" (hand-painted on small boards) that he gave to some students also demonstrate a touch of whimsy. For many years, it was a point of honor to have been educated by Leavitt, and many of his students went on to become successful farmers (like Smith Neal, one of whose awards is here shown), as well as teachers (like Isaiah Orne of Wolfeboro). In regard to churchgoing, Leavitt was a member of no church and likely disagreed with organized religion as it was then practiced, but his wife, Judith, was, and he sometimes sat with her during religious events.

Reward of Merit painted by Dudley Leavitt for Smith Neal, circa 1820, from Mary Hanaford's *Family Records*.

When he was not teaching, Leavitt remained as busy as a man can be. He spent much time studying and writing, especially in the subject of astronomy, and the work he produced was regularly discussed by the academic community at large in New England and beyond, including at the American Philosophical Society and the American Academy of Arts and Sciences. Ironically, his works were so prolific that when he slowed down a bit after closing his school in 1846, reports began to circulate that he had died, and he was forced to refute that fact in his 1851 edition of the almanac (which retained the old-fashioned spelling of "almanack" during its entire run under his guidance). In a further bit of irony, Leavitt dropped dead in his house, after his 1851 almanac was published, on September 20, 1851. Two days later, even the *New York Times* published a brief obituary, stating, "Dudley Leavitt, the veteran almanac maker, died this morning." Now, while you might think that Leavitt was just a man of science and education, he was more than even that. He was also an avid farmer who worked his land daily right up until the time he died and was up to date on the latest farming information, as only befitted a man of education. Thus, when you

The author with a copy of *Leavitt's Farmer's Almanack* for 1851, at the grave site of Dudley Leavitt in Meredith.

read his articles or tidbits about when Indian corn and potatoes are "fit to harvest," the best way to preserve "beets, carrots, and other roots" or the best ways "to trap foxes" (all found in his 1851 almanac), you realize that this is a man speaking from experience. After Leavitt's death, his almanac continued in publication well into the twentieth century, first under the guidance of his relative William Leavitt, who also helped with astronomical calculations. Dudley and Judith Leavitt had eleven children, two of whom died young, leaving many descendants in the area, which accounts for the several small Leavitt cemeteries in Meredith today.

The importance of Dudley Leavitt to the Lakes Region and beyond cannot be overstated. He was an outstanding academic, a renowned teacher and the author of a famed publication that probably sold hundreds of thousands of copies during his lifetime, including some sixty thousand copies in 1846 alone. Dog-eared and well-worn copies of his almanac can even be purchased to this day for but a small price, a testament to Leavitt's legacy. I don't know about you, but I'm keeping my copy hanging by its string in my kitchen, near my old wood stove. Just in case.

CHAPTER 5

THE INDIAN GRAVE BY THE LAKE

Perhaps New Hampshire state archaeologist Dr. Richard Boisvert, in his conversation with writer Mark Dionne, said it best when it comes to Native American historical sites, especially in the Lakes Region: "We don't have those obvious, flashy sites here in New Hampshire....By and large, if you go somewhere in New Hampshire and it looks really nice and you'd like to live there, you're not the first one to have that idea." One of the many places that fits this bill is Melvin Village, part of the town of Tuftonboro, its center being close to the spot where the Melvin River empties into Lake Winnipesaukee. One of the interesting things to be seen at this site, located adjacent to the Melvin Village Community Church, is a simple yet elegant sign that reads, "The Grave by the Lake" and is topped by a silhouette of an Indian archer. Many older locals can tell you what the sign signifies for sure, but many of those who are younger have no clue, some believing it refers to the cemetery behind the church. In fact, it was here in 1808 (some sources state the year as 1817), when the channel of the river was being widened, that the skeletal remains of a Native American were found. But these were not just any remains, for buried in the sandy soil were remains indicative of a man who stood over seven feet tall, his jawbone alone larger than the face of an ordinary man. What became of these remains is unknown, so nothing of this discovery's details can be verified. State archaeologists believe that the details as to size are quite possibly in error, but no one really knows. Other Native American artifacts, as in all other towns surrounding the lake, have also been discovered in Tuftonboro, according to early historian John

The roadside sign for the Indian Grave by the Lake, with the Melvin Village Community Church behind.

Haley, including an artificial mound the size of a regular grave, with tightly packed stones. It was once marked with a headstone indicating that a chief was buried there.

This site, too, is gone, but it was the grave uncovered by the Melvin River that would later catch the imagination of one of New England's greatest poets, John Greenleaf Whittier. He was a frequent summer visitor to the lake, residing in Center Harbor but making frequent forays around the area. His twenty-six-stanza poem "The Grave by the Lake," written in 1865 and first published in the *Atlantic Monthly*, later published in his book of poems titled *Tent on the Beach* in 1867, came nearly sixty years after the discovery of the remains and was inspired by local lore and legend. The publication of this poem would, over the ensuing years, inspire many visitors to this site, and in 1955, the Ley family placed a granite marker here. As in so many places in New Hampshire and the rest of America, long before the white man came and established their own church cemetery in this most beautiful of spots, Native Americans were the first to do so. The remains uncovered here likely belonged to a member of the Ossipee tribe, who seem to have buried their dead in mounded configurations, including one such site, very large in size, in the neighboring town of Ossipee. This mound was said to have been excavated around 1800 and included some eight hundred burials by estimate, the bodies tightly packed in a sitting position. Sadly, none of these sites were preserved into modern times, so the nature of these accounts cannot be verified. However, we do know, especially through archaeological digs across the lake at the Weirs, that Native Americans were here thousands of years before we arrived. To that end, let us honor them as we gaze across the lake in Melvin Village, keeping in our thoughts the haunting words of John Greenleaf Whittier, which begin with this stanza:

> *Where the Great Lake's sunny smiles*
> *Dimple round its hundred isles,*
> *And the mountain's granite ledge*
> *Cleaves the water like a ledge,*
> *Ringed about with smooth, gray stones,*
> *Rest the giant's mighty bones.*

Continues on with:

> *Where be now these silent hosts?*
> *Where the camping-ground of ghosts?*
> *Where the spectral conscripts led?*
> *To the white tents of the dead?*
> *What strange shore or chartless sea*
> *Holds the awful mystery?*

And ends:

> *Keep, O pleasant Melvin stream,*
> *Thy sweet laugh in shade and gleam!*
> *On the Indian's grassy tomb*
> *Swing, O flowers, your bells of bloom!*
> *Deep below, as high above,*
> *Sweeps the circle of God's love.*

CHAPTER 6

INDUSTRY BEFORE TOURISM

L ong before the advent of the tourist-based economy on which the Lake Winnipesaukee area depends today, it was local industry and manufacturing that was the lifeblood of the region. The evidence of this early industrial activity, mostly in the form of mills, as well as associated railroad lines and commercial shipping on the lake, has largely vanished, and what sites do remain are easy for residents and visitors alike to overlook. The three interesting historic sites discussed below, where mill manufacturing activity dating back to the 1760s took place, are hidden in plain sight and well worthy of a closer look.

The most historic of these sites, the Belknap and Busiel mills, are found in the city of Laconia, once a part of Meredith Bridge and several other neighboring communities until its incorporation in 1855. To this day, it is the only Lakes Region city that retains a significant manufacturing base. The Belknap Mill, located along the Winnipesaukee River at 25 Beacon Street East, is significant today as the oldest unaltered brick textile mill in the country, as well as the only surviving building that represents the first stage of the Industrial Revolution in America. For these reasons, as well as the fact that it has been a museum since 1991, the Belknap Mill is also likely the best known of the surviving mill complexes in the area. As a resident of the Lakes Region, I've driven by this site many times and knew of its existence and a little of its history, but it took me fifteen years to pay it a full-on visit. Once I did take the time to visit, however, I found the Belknap Mill immensely interesting. The first mill structure on this site was constructed of wood in

1811 and burned down in 1823. However, the site was too beneficial for the water power it offered to leave vacant for long, and soon enough, the current mill building was under construction, beginning in 1823 and completed in full by 1828. The mill is a brick post-and-beam structure whose exterior has remained largely unaltered since its completion in 1828. Interestingly, the bell in the mill tower, which signaled the beginning and end of the working day for the millworkers, was cast in Medway, Massachusetts, by well-known bellmaker George Holbrook (once an apprentice to Paul Revere) from the metal of the original bell from the 1811-built structure. The first mill was owned by the Meredith Cotton and Woolen Manufacturing Company, but by 1831, the new mill was owned by the Avery Factory Company, named after the agent who operated the mill. At the beginning of the Civil War in 1861, the prosperous mill was owned by Robert Bailey and Kendall Gleason of Lawrence, Massachusetts. It was also in this year that the factory converted from weaving to knitting machinery, a revolutionary change, employing a circular knitting machine that allowed the company to manufacture untold quantities of seamless hosiery and bags. While this mill seems at first glance to have been a large operation, in comparison to the giant textile mills that developed in Manchester and Dover, New Hampshire, it was actually quite small and today is a rare survivor of the small-scale manufacturing activities that took place in many rural New England communities. Nonetheless, the mill was an important employer in Laconia and provided work and economic opportunities for thousands of women during its years of operations.

In 1918, the mill was modernized with the addition of a hydropower plant at the rear, its three giant turbine engines and associated machinery costing $100,000 to provide power for the mill's machinery and lighting system. This system remained in use up to 1969, and even into the 1980s it could have been brought online again if needed. Indeed, it is the machinery inside this old mill that provides the real hidden history of local manufacturing. The hydropower plant components are massive in size and impressive to see, but equally interesting is the large collection of knitting machines to be found on display on the main factory floor. Frankly, I have never given much thought to how socks, or any clothing for that matter, are made, but these machines, which are old but nonetheless quite complex and represented the newest in technology at the time, are fascinating to look at even though they sit silently, their manufacturing days long gone. It's no wonder that this mill museum entertains and educates many school-age children. In fact, socks were produced at the Belknap Mill right up until its closure in 1969. Following this, the mill was nearly demolished, but it was eventually saved,

The Belknap Mill in Laconia, circa 1950s.

added to the National Register of Historic Places in 1972 and subsequently turned into a museum. The Belknap Mill Society raised over $500,000 to purchase and preserve the site. When you visit this site, you will also notice the neighboring Busiel Mill, which was built in 1853 by John Busiel, the father of New Hampshire governor Charles Busiel, and expanded into an impressive three-and-a-half-story complex by 1882. Over the years, a wide variety of manufactured goods were produced here, including hosiery, clocks and organs, and at one time it was one of the largest hosiery manufacturers in New Hampshire. While the Belknap Mill was built of standard building materials, it did have improvements in its building to decrease fire dangers, and the Busiel Mill is notable, in addition to its massive size, for continuing such modern industrial safety construction techniques with the adoption of so-called slow-burn floor framing to make it more fire-safe. Today, the mill has been converted to office business space.

Just a short distance away from Laconia to the west is the town of Meredith. Here, at 312 Daniel Webster Highway (U.S. Route 3), you will find our next historic manufacturing site. Today, the complex, which includes an inn and a grouping of shops and restaurants, is called the Mill Falls Marketplace. While today it is a charming retail tourist site, it actually got its start, beginning about 1818, as a modern industrial complex. It was here in

Meredith Village—on the land bounded to the east by Dover Street, to the north and west by Main Street and dropping down to modern-day Daniel Webster Highway and the shores of Lake Winnipesaukee just beyond—that John Bond Swasey inherited ninety-five acres of land from his father, Benjamin Swasey. In the late 1810s, he conceived the project of building a canal from Lake Waukewan, alongside which John Bond Swasey Park may be found today, which carried water to a point where the land drops sharply to the lake below, creating a powerful waterfall that dropped some forty feet, creating a great source of mill power. The rock-lined canal, a portion of which can be easily seen from Main Street today, ran some six hundred feet, carrying water under the street and to the mill falls area. It was completed by about 1818, a nice bit of engineering. All of the mills first established here, including a sawmill, a gristmill and a cotton mill, were owned by Swasey and were the source of his local business empire, and it is said that his artificial mill falls were one of the best in the entire state. After his death in 1828, the so-called Mill Lot lands were sold to Captain Daniel Smith of neighboring New Hampton in 1830 by Swasey's wife.

In 1834, the mill for the Meredith Cotton and Woolen Company was built. This company lasted but a short time, the mill subsequently out of business and idle by 1850 until Seneca Ladd, a prominent man who later established the Meredith Village Savings Bank, leased the cotton mill and here made pianos and melodeons (a trade he had previously worked at in Boston). Ladd was later prominent in persuading Samuel Hodgson to establish a mill here. In 1855, Smith sold the lands to his son James Smith for $6,000 (the equivalent of over $179,000 in 2020). A short time later, in 1858, Joseph Ela and his partners formed the Meredith Mechanics Association and bought the buildings and water rights to the falls area from Smith for $15,000. They subsequently upgraded and modernized the waterway and leased the space in the area to attract new mill companies, bringing a great amount of business to the area. Indeed, it's hard to believe that within the bounds of Dover and Main Streets, today a quaint village area, there was once a sizeable industrial complex, the chief reminders of which today are the renovated mill building itself, the canal that brings water to the falls and the impressive waterfall itself, today the centerpiece of the site. The Meredith Mechanics Association dominated for some thirty years until a fire in 1889 destroyed the largest mill, the one leased by the Hodgson Hosiery Company, owned by Englishman Samuel Hodgson since 1876 and employing 160 workers. This loss devastated the local economy, as the mill was the largest employer in town. The following year, the forward-thinking Joseph Ela died, and the association came to an end. The Mill Lot property was purchased by Hodgson for $12,500 and turned into the Meredith Water Power Company. There, the Atlas Linen Company operated until its closure in 1907. In 1917, the Mill Lot was sold to the Meredith Linen Mills for $25,000, and from then on out, textiles and linens were primarily produced there until it was shuttered in the 1940s. The mill was later, in 1951, acquired by a company that manufactured asbestos textiles and would continue in this unfortunate role, with another change of ownership in 1962, for some thirty years before its final closure in 1982. Luckily, the mill saw new life when it was purchased by a local developer and fully renovated and repurposed into its current role as an inn and retail space beginning in 1984. Few people realize all of the goods that were produced by the water power at this site for over 160 years, in the days when industry reigned supreme.

Our final hidden industrial gem is located on the other side of the lake in the town of Wolfeboro, which today, like Meredith, is seldom thought of for its manufacturing history. However, the site at Wolfeboro Falls, where the Smith River empties into Lake Winnipesaukee at Back Bay, was in use

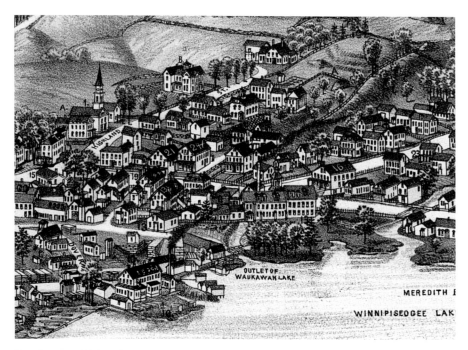

Detail, map of Meredith, 1889. The building numbered 13 is the Meredith Mechanics Association's mill, just above and to the left of the Waukawan Lake outlet.

The Mill Falls Market Place today, whose old spillway (*at left*) still empties into Lake Winnipesaukee just a short distance away.

for this purpose for over two hundred years. The remnants of the last mill at Wolfeboro Falls can be viewed via the Russell C. Chase Bridge Falls Path, beginning behind the old railroad station on Railroad Avenue in downtown Wolfeboro. The site can also be accessed at the opposite end, with parking available in a small lot at 90 Center Street. This industrial part of Wolfeboro got its start in 1769, when George Meserve built a sawmill in the area, and it is interesting to note that even Royal Governor John Wentworth, with his summer estate just to the north on Lake Wentworth, had an interest in erecting a mill here. However, he was beaten to the punch, the water rights to the falls, as well as one hundred acres of surrounding land, having already been granted to David Sewall and Ami Cutter. Upon hearing of the governor's interest, Sewall wrote a letter to his partner in November 1774, asking Cutter to "inquire into the matter… and prevent our entering into a controversy with his Excellence." Whether Cutter, a noted Portsmouth physician who was a friend of Wentworth's, ever had such a discussion is unknown, but months later, the advent of the American Revolution solved the matter for good when Wentworth left New Hampshire, never to return.

In the succeeding years, there were a number of mills at Wolfeboro Falls, including an excelsior mill owned by Frank Hutchins beginning in 1889 and the mill owned by Oliver P. Berry in 1885, which made untold quantities of axe and other tool handles before turning to excelsior in 1899. By 1901, there were three factories at the falls making excelsior and employing about forty men. Yet another factory at the falls, that owned by Lorenzo Horne, made piano stools. As can be seen, excelsior by far was the most prominent and longest-lasting product manufactured here well into the twentieth century. Few today know what this product is, but the answer is simple; it is basically shaved or shredded wood that was used as packing material for fragile goods long before the days of bubble wrap but was also used as stuffing for furniture cushions and even teddy bears. Tons of excelsior were produced at Wolfeboro Falls well into the 1970s, including later being used by a company that shipped live baby chicks.

The remnants of the mill that can be seen today were once part of the O.P. Berry Company and, lastly, the Smith River Company. Once the mill closed for good in the late 1970s, it stood idle and, not surprisingly, was subject to vandalism. The vacant mill suffered a major fire in 1985 and another in 1994, so little is left of its former glory, but enough is left to give one a good idea of the importance of the falls. Interesting survivals include the towering smokestack, the foundation of one building and one surviving powerhouse building. The falls themselves are impressive when roaring at full capacity, though lodged in the mill race is a toppled metal smokestack from one of the burned buildings. Another interesting aspect of this site is the evidence of the railroad tracks that once ran on this path, freight trains

The ruins of the O.P. Berry mill at Wolfeboro Falls, as seen from the Russell Chase Bridge-Falls Path.

Ruins of the O.P. Berry mill at Wolfeboro Falls. The outlet of the Smith River is nearly dried up, exposing the fallen-down smokestack.

both bringing in raw materials and carrying out finished product for many decades, with service on the line ending for good in the 1980s.

So, what is today a path for recreation and exercise in Wolfeboro was once an economic lifeline upon which many local families depended on for their livelihood long before tourism came along. Now, if you live in this area, maybe that ancient teddy bear you have packed away in the attic or your antique chair is filled with excelsior that came from Wolfeboro. You never know!

CHAPTER 7

LIGHTNING STRIKES IN EAST ALTON

Throughout the eastern end of Lake Winnipesaukee, especially in Wolfeboro, Alton, Ossipee and Tuftonboro, one can find while traveling the backroads small rural churches tucked away into the landscape. Some remain active year round, but most are either summer churches or historic church buildings whose members have long since passed on. One such structure in the last category, the old East Alton Meeting House, home of the Free Will Baptist Church, may be found in East Alton, located at 347 Drew Hill Road, just north of Gilman's Corner Road. It was built sometime between 1807 and 1821, but records are fragmentary, and no one knows for sure. For over fifty years, it was the home of an active church organization, but by the late nineteenth century, as Alton Village grew and two new churches were built there, this church went into a slow decline. It got down to just a few members and was essentially extinguished in 1907 when its last member died, though no settled minister had preached there since 1883. Languishing in this rural area, it fell into disrepair and was in danger of being lost until the East Alton Community Association organized in the late 1920s and raised the needed funds to restore and maintain the church structure. Historic structures like this are a reminder of the many small communities that existed in the area, only to fade away as settlement patterns changed. It is easy to forget sometimes that they were the heart of the community and are today the only tangible representation of the triumphs and tragedies that individuals like those in early East Alton endured. Indeed, life was hard in the first decades of the nineteenth century in the Lakes Region as communities were being carved out of the wilderness and the "lake life" existence so many of us enjoy today was not yet possible.

Oftentimes we have to use our imagination, coupled with our learned historical knowledge, to gauge what life must have been like for these early settlers, but for this church, surviving church records can give us a glimpse into members' social lives and the events that rocked their world. This church got its start in January 1803, and records were kept from the very beginning, mostly documenting religious affairs and meetings, which often took place in members' homes, even after their church was built. Records for around the time that this church was built portray the ups and downs of the community in both quaint and graphic fashion. On September 4, 1820, while the church members were meeting, "the south wind flow'd a Heavenly gale, and the fogg [sic] & mists fled a way and the church appeared to be adjourning to the land of rest and glory." As we shall see, the weather would soon play a larger part in the history of this church. During the years from late 1821 to early 1824, relations between and among members would ebb and flow.

In November 1821, the church met "but did not experience the presence of the Lord as they had at times before. Reports from the visiting committee were unfavorable and agree to reject John Garland & wife from the fellowship of the church." No reason for this rejection was given. On January 19, 1822, the church members met and "parted without any union or reconciliation." On March 6, 1822, "the brethren that met had a good season and parted in peace." Sadly, whatever troubles there may have been that were overcome in that "good season" would end within a year.

In March 1823, "the church experienced great trials and difficulties" for reasons unknown. January 1824 "commence[d] without any revival in religion but a continuation of trials." Many members departed the church at this time, some moving elsewhere, others perhaps due to leaving the church, either voluntarily or by church decree. The nature of these difficulties went unspecified for the reason "that they may be buried in the ruin of time." For those members of the church in good standing who departed voluntarily, their absence left a void in the church.

However, it was in the year 1825 that this church would see its greatest trials, ones that shocked the community. It all began on a summer day, August 6, a Friday afternoon, when "Brother Moses Glidden's wife was killed by a stream of lightning" on an otherwise clear day while she was out working in the family field. Note that Glidden's wife, Sarah Glidden (born 1784), is not referred to by name, nor was she described as "sister," meaning that she was not a member of the church. In response to this tragedy,

> *The shock was solemn and awful, the people appeared awakened and many who had not pray'd many years began to pray the following evening as was related in their experience afterwards. Her remains were committed to the house appointed for all living on the sabbath after in presence of a very solemn assembly. After this, the meetings were very full and crowded and many thought on their ways and made haste & delayed not to do the commands, broke off their sins by righteousness and their iniquities by returning to the Lord and some obtained deliverance in their minds. And about the last of the month the awakening became general....Meetings were now held almost every evening in the week and the congregation was so large that no dwelling house could hold the people, therefore they were obliged to repair to the meetinghouse and it was well filled every evening and the power of the Lord was present and almost every meeting awful and Glorious.*

This lone tragedy was perhaps the end to a long period of suffering for the church members, as "from the 27th of November 1824 to July 1825 it pleased the Lord to visit this Church & People with a great sickness and Mortality," causing nine people to die, including three children of the Edgerley family. What may have brought the Lord's displeasure on their community they did not know, but did Sarah Glidden have anything to do with these events? In fact, nothing more after her burial is mentioned about Glidden in church records, but her death by lightning strike has remained a part of Alton's oral history, with many folks believing that Glidden may have been a witch. Their case is bolstered by the fact that her grave, which lies on private property nearby and is inaccessible to the general public, is not only marked by a typical headstone and footstone, but the area in between is covered by a large stone slab. No other grave site in this area is so covered, and it is worth noting that it was a practice in early colonial times in New England to cover the graves of suspected witches in this manner so that their bodies could not rise up at night and haunt the living. It is also true that no "mortality" so great as that which occurred just before her death is noted again in church records. So, there you have it—a witch in East Alton who met her end at the hands of God in an unsuspecting moment. Of course, the witch question can never be answered or proven, and it seems unfair (though admittedly less entertaining) to Sarah Glidden to characterize her as such. Her husband, Moses Glidden, was a member in good standing in the church for years

The East Alton Meeting House, where members of the Free Will Baptist Church—
including Moses Glidden, but not his wife—worshipped for many years.

afterward. The monthly meeting was held at his house in November 1830, despite "the weather being cold & stormy," and in September 1834, he was in charge of getting the wine for "communion season." Nothing about his wife is ever mentioned. Whether Sarah Glidden was an immoral person we cannot know, but there is no evidence for such. Could it be that she was just an independent-minded woman who did not care to be bound by the restrictions of the male-dominated church and preferred to live life as best as she could on her own terms?

In fact, what scant evidence there is in church records shows that some women did have their difficulties. Way back in the church's early years, in September 1806, "Sister" Sarah York was castigated for "thy long absence from us and the reproach that thy light and vain conduct hath brought upon the course of religion." Interestingly, fifteen years after the death of Sarah Glidden, on December 16, 1840, a young woman named Lois Glidden, age twenty-eight, was "dismissed from the Fellowship of this church" for reasons unknown. While her relationship to Sarah is unknown, perhaps the Glidden women of East Alton were all a bit spirited. As a final note, not far away, in Riverside Cemetery, in its far southeastern end, may be found the graves of

The burial site of Sarah Glidden in East Alton. It is covered by a stone slab, leading to legends claiming her to be a witch.

The lightning bolt–themed (seen in each upper corner) gravestone of Abraham Edgerly (1815–1824), Riverside Cemetery, Alton.

the three children of the Edgerley family, all of whom died between October 1824 and January 1825. Their gravestones were likely placed sometime in late 1825. They, too, were called out of this world suddenly by illness, and all have identical motifs on the corners of their gravestones that resemble streaks of lightning. These one-of-a kind gravestones offer additional artistic proof that the lightning bolt that struck Sarah Glidden down lay heavily on everyone's minds.

The above accounts highlight just a few of the events in the lives of the members of the church in East Alton. They are all long gone now, and though some descendants remain in the area, the church building that was one of the focal parts of their lives remains. It is a beautifully maintained example of a rural church structure that has Greek Revival stylistic details and is pleasing to the eye, but it is those life events that took place both within its walls and within a few square miles of rural countryside that are the real hidden history.

CHAPTER 8

THE END OF THE WORLD IN GILFORD

Probably the most exclusive island in Lake Winnipesaukee is Governors Island, but where today it is the site of multimillion-dollar homes and a rich lake-life lifestyle, it wasn't always that way. Just one of six islands connected to the mainland by a bridge, it was once entirely owned by the Davis family of Gilford. And it was here, between March 21, 1843, and March 21, 1844, that they waited in great anticipation for the end of the world. The island, already known by its current name, was granted to Royal Governor John Wentworth in 1772 and was probably named after his uncle and predecessor Royal Governor Benning Wentworth. However, with the advent of the Revolutionary War, Governor Wentworth was forced to depart New Hampshire in 1775, leaving behind his holdings in Wolfeboro, as well as Governors Island. Confiscated by the new state, it was subsequently sold to Bostonian John Cushing in 1780 and thereafter in 1788 to Governor John Langdon, a most fitting sale if ever there was one. Langdon, in turn, sold it to a Revolutionary War soldier, Lemuel Mason of Alton, in 1797, and he sold it to Eleazer Davis of Gilmanton (later Gilford with the incorporation of the town in 1812). The island would stay in the Davis family for sixty years, and it was Nathaniel Davis (1778–1857), the son of Eleazer, who would be the driving force in the family for years. It was said that he was "a stalwart and commanding personage, and exercised his gifts as a leader in matters of free church order in preaching and public discussion." This statement gives us an idea of Davis's independent spirit, the historian going on to say, "The family largely embraced Miller's doctrine, though at first following one of Osgood

Portrait of William Miller, visitor to Governors Island. From Bliss's *Memoirs of William Miller*, 1858.

of anti-church government sentiment." This also gives us some insight into "Island" Davis (as he was nicknamed) and his radical religious beliefs. Jacob Osgood, a New Hampshire native, taught that anything established by man was the work of the devil and that man should withdraw from government altogether, pay no taxes, not partake in any military service and not vote. How long Nathaniel Davis held these views is unknown, but there is no evidence that he went to the extremes that fervent Osgoodites did, including growing their hair long, not bathing or washing and dressing in old-fashioned clothes. However, it does seem that Davis was open to less than traditional religious views. Thus, enters the picture one William Miller (1782–1849), a Baptist preacher from Low Hampton, New York, who was a founder of the Adventist religion in America. Over the early years of his career, after studying the Bible intently, Miller stated publicly:

> *I believe that when Christ comes, he will destroy the bodies of the living wicked by fire, as those of the old were destroyed by water, and shut up their souls in the pit of woe until their resurrection unto damnation.*
>
> *I believe when the earth is cleansed by fire, that Christ and his saints will then take possession of the earth and dwell there forever.*

This coming of Christ struck a chord with many in the northeastern United States, and Miller went on extensive speaking tours all through New England and New York beginning in the late 1830s, first coming to New Hampshire to speak at Exeter in November 1839 and again in January 1840, as well as Portsmouth and Deerfield in 1840 and Dover in December 1841. One historian stated that Miller held a camp meeting in Gilford in 1840, but this is not mentioned in Miller's detailed biography. If 1840 was the year that Nathaniel Davis took on the beliefs of Miller, he may have visited one of these other events. However, it was William Miller's tour of New Hampshire in July 1843 that really excited his followers to a great degree. He started out in Claremont and then went to Springfield, Wilmot, Andover and Franklin. These were all one-day affairs, but from July 21 to 24, he visited Gilford, and his three-day stay with Davis on Governors Island was the longest of any of his New Hampshire stays before continuing on to Concord. These meetings were wildly enthusiastic and ripe with emotion, which was not Miller's desire at all, his biographer stating, "During this tour, Mr. Miller was much pained by witnessing a tendency to fanaticism on the part of some who held his views." Whether the folks in Gilford, or the Davis family in particular, were some of these fanatics is not known. However, what is known is that Davis and his family on Governors Island, like many who fervently believed in Miller's views, turned away from the outside world, ceasing to tend to all but the barest of worldly affairs, instead praying and communing with like-minded family members and friends and hopefully waiting for the appearance of Christ. As the year went on, it is said that many of Miller's followers failed to tend to their crops and were dependent on kindly town members to survive, but once again, we don't know about the Davis family, who made a living by farming. However, Millerism was more active in Gilford by all accounts than most other Lakes Region towns.

In the end, the appointed day of Christ's coming, March 21, 1844, came and went, and nothing happened. Miller would later say, "I confess my error, and acknowledge my disappointment; yet I still believe that the day of the Lord is near, even at the door; and I exhort you, my brethren, to be watchful." Sadly, for them, this day would never come, and Miller paid his last visit to New Hampshire during a camp visit in Derry in October 1844. He later became blind and limited in his travels prior to his death.

As for Nathaniel Davis on Governors Island, whether he remained "watchful" until the end of his days is unknown. After his death in 1857, his sons Franklin and Eleazer Davis sold Governors Island to George Smith of Meredith and David Plummer of Concord, who in turn in 1872 sold

The Davis family cemetery on Governors Island, where Nathaniel "Island" Davis is buried.

it to Isaac Merrill and Henry Brown of Gilford. In 1882, these men sold the island to the man who is best known today as its former owner, Stilson Hutchins, the founder and editor of the *Washington Post*. Here he built his large stone mansion in 1885, thereby beginning the transformation of the island, and entertained several presidents here over the years. The property remained in the family until its sale to Clifford Hayes in 1928, and after he went bankrupt during the Great Depression, it was acquired in 1935 by the Governors Island Club, which retains control of the island to this day. Today, perhaps the only remnant of the Davis family on the island is the family cemetery, where Millerite Nathaniel "Island" Davis is buried. It's hard to believe, though, as you drive around this wooded island and view its elaborate homes, that it was once a place where the end of the world was fervently hoped and prayed for.

Chapter 9

College Sports Get Their Start in Center Harbor

I f you love college sports, whether it's a March Madness basketball game or a college football Saturday, this next bit of history may surprise you. The first ever intercollegiate sporting match actually took place not on a weekend day but on a Tuesday afternoon in, of all places, Center Harbor, New Hampshire, on August 3, 1852. And it didn't involve one of the so-called major college sporting events that most everyone thinks of today that are televised but the sport of rowing (sometimes called "crew"). It was on a summer weekday afternoon that the rowing clubs of Harvard and Yale inaugurated college sports with a match on Lake Winnipesaukee in the waters off Center Harbor, long before football, basketball and baseball were established on college campuses. But how did such an event come to pass? Well, it all started on a June train ride in Laconia at the Weirs, when Boston, Concord and Montreal Railroad superintendent James Elkins took a seat next to a friend of his, James Whiton Jr. The two young men had been classmates together at Boston Latin before heading their separate ways, with Whiton going to Yale. Interestingly, Whiton's father, James Whiton Sr., was a director for the railroad, and the family had ties to the Lakes Region and visited often. During the train ride, the younger Whiton commented to Elkins as they were passing the lake at the Weirs that the waters there would be a good place to hold a regatta. Whiton, in fact, was the bow oarsman for the Yale rowing club and their boat *Undine*, so he had some experience under his belt. Upon hearing Whiton's comments, Superintendent Elkins had an idea. Why not hold a match between the Yale and Harvard rowing clubs on Lake Winnipesaukee? He told Whiton that if the club at Yale could get Harvard to agree to a match, both clubs would be transported to the lake and housed and fed, all at the expense of the railroad. You see, the Boston, Concord and Montreal was a relatively new railroad, established in 1844, and by early 1850, it had just made it to the northern edge of the Lakes Region. Constantly striving to increase ridership, Elkins saw a chance in this event to draw thousands of people via his railroad to the lake, perhaps even make a tradition of it. Despite the younger Whiton's enthusiasm for the match, the question remained: would Harvard accept the challenge? Whiton's first attempt at a challenge was not accepted, largely because the annual commencement for Harvard was taking place soon, in early July, while Yale's commencement came several weeks later. On a second attempt at the challenge, Whiton spoke with his friend Joseph Brown, who was a rower on the Harvard club, and he was able to talk his team members into accepting the challenge. The match, however, could not take place until after Yale's commencement on July 29.

It should be noted that before this match, rowing, like most early sports on campus, was a club activity, where young men at the school banded together to row for fun. The first such college club was formed at Yale in 1843. There was no coach, no training schedule, no strict match schedules—it was all a leisure activity. It was at Harvard in 1845 that a group of juniors and the Oneida Club challenged the seniors to a rowing match, with the seniors then forming their own organization, the Iris Boat Club. The juniors won the match with their eight-oared "barge" named the *Oneida*—the same craft that they would use against Yale on Lake Winnipesaukee seven years later. Interestingly, the boats used by these clubs in 1852 on Lake Winnipesaukee were more like whaleboats or barges, big and stout, and nothing like the shells used today, which are sleek and streamlined, though changes in their design would soon be coming.

For the grand event on Lake Winnipesaukee, with the entire trip lasting eight days, which the *New York Times* predicted would pass without much notice, the Harvard club fielded one boat, the *Oneida*, with a crew of nine, as well as several alternates, so eleven men in all. In contrast, Yale sent thirty men in three squads for the boats *Undine*, *Shawmut* and *Atalanta*, the latter (loaned by a New York club) to be disqualified from the race for its vastly different form. The match overall was viewed by most club members as a "jolly lark," a chance to get away from school on an all-expenses paid trip, though three members on the Harvard side elected not to come and had to be replaced. Maybe they had other plans, or perhaps they'd rather spend time at home with their families or girlfriends. Who knows, but whatever the case may have been, they missed out on what would turn out to be a historic opportunity. In any case, the men from Yale and Harvard met at the Concord, New Hampshire railroad depot on Friday, July 30, and then took the train to the Weirs. Here, they did some practice rowing on Saturday, but on Sunday, August 1, the Sabbath was strictly observed, as was customary then in New England. At some point, the clubs took the steamer *Lady of the Lake* to Center Harbor, where they stayed at the famed Senter House Hotel. Meanwhile, the railroad and its agents had tacked up posters for the event far and wide in the Lakes Region, hoping to gain business from the event, and heavily promoted the match. On Monday, August 2, both teams practiced rowing in the waters off Center Harbor, though it appeared to some observers that the Yale men were taking things a bit more seriously.

The day of the regatta, August 3, 1852, dawned bright and sunny, with a slight breeze, a perfect summer day. Several practice races were held in the early part of the day, with the Harvard club winning, led by their captain and coxswain, Joseph Brown. Later in the afternoon, both clubs took a break, with the Harvard men having a cigar and some mineral water, as well as a large meal, in the hours before the official race, which was to commence at 4:00 p.m. Prior to the race, the *Oneida*, *Undine* and *Shawmut* were towed to the starting line by a horse-boat, a typical commercial craft on the lake that was powered by a horse on a treadmill, which, in turn, powered a paddle-wheel—a strange craft indeed. The sole Harvard team was decked out in uniforms of red, white and blue, while Yale's *Shawmut* crew was dressed in blue and white and the *Undine* crew was dressed in red and white. All around them, at a safe distance, were spectators and observers, while on one boat the Concord Mechanics Association Brass Band (still in existence today) was providing musical entertainment. The two-mile race started promptly at 4:00 p.m., with Harvard's *Oneida* leading by one length, but in the end, they surged ahead, beating *Shawmut* by two lengths and *Undine* by about four. It was all over in about ten minutes. Once ashore, the band played, speeches were made and, with the 1852 Democratic presidential candidate, New Hampshire's own General Franklin Pierce, looking on, a set of trophy oars, made of black walnut and inscribed in silver, was presented to the Harvard crew.

Accounts vary, but the match was witnessed by anywhere from several hundred up to as many as one thousand spectators. Whatever the numbers were, the event in the end did not prove to be a financial boom for the railroad. The next day, the teams traveled to Wolfeboro to hold another regatta, but a "drenching" rain prevailed on that day, so the event was canceled. When the rain finally did let up a bit, the clubs gave a rowing demonstration "for the gratification of the townspeople," and the trophy boathook intended for that day's victor, also inscribed in silver, was instead given to the crew of the *Shawmut*, the prior day's runner-up. With the end of their regatta, the first ever intercollegiate sporting event, the men from Harvard and Yale stayed in the area, doing some relaxing and sightseeing before returning home by train the following Saturday.

In the aftermath of this event, no regatta would take place again in New Hampshire, and the next one would be delayed until 1855, this time taking place at Springfield, Massachusetts. In that 1855 match, Harvard's *Oneida* was again the victor. The boat was later sold to the Dartmouth University rowing club in 1856 and lost within a short time when it was washed over a dam on the Connecticut River. Interestingly, as author Ronald Smith has pointed out, college athletics as we know them today, with schedules, coaches and preparation, would become the norm within a decade, and it may even be said that the New Hampshire event had wider implications for college sports in general regarding student eligibility. Harvard's coxswain in 1852, James Brown, was again the team leader in 1855, even though he had graduated in 1853, and as Smith notes, the eligibility of graduates would remain a sore spot for many decades thereafter. And finally, what about those trophy oars? If you think they're locked away in some Harvard trophy cabinet as a still-valued prize, you'd be wrong. These oars were eventually

No. 198—Lake Winnipesaukee—from Senter House, Center Harbor.

A stereoscopic view of Lake Winnipesaukee from Center Harbor, the site of the first Harvard-Yale regatta.

lost, only to be rediscovered about 2006—holding up an old basement window in a Medford, Massachusetts home that had just been sold. Talk about basement treasures! The new owner, recognizing their historic nature, later put them on eBay for sale at the incredible price of $30 million but had no takers. To put that asking price in perspective, the famed Honus Wagner baseball card is valued at $1 million, while the record-setting homerun baseball hit by Mark McGwire sold for $3 million. The trophy oars were even offered to Harvard directly, for the same exorbitant price, which, not surprisingly, Harvard refused to pay. At this writing, as far as is known, these oars are still in private hands, which shows that, while you can put a price on Lake Winnipesaukee history, it doesn't always mean that someone will pay it. Maybe someday these oars will end up in one of their rightful homes, perhaps even the Center Harbor Historical Society, but I'm not going to bet on that outcome.

CHAPTER 10

THE WARHORSES OF THE TWELFTH

Those of us who have had a favorite animal in our life, a beloved dog or cat or horse, will perhaps understand this story the most. Today, pets are ubiquitous to our world, but so, too, were they to our ancestors in the nineteenth century. While dogs were favored pets even back then for many men, perhaps the most important animal was the horse, which not only served as a means of getting from one place to another but also was a constant companion in daily life. However, the relationship between man and horse was amplified in times of war, in which countless military men ever since the advent of mounted warfare have depended on their trusty steeds to carry them through battle safely. Alexander the Great had his Bucephalus (noted for one blue eye), Napoleon had his Arabian stallion Marengo and George Washington rode a half-Arabian named Blueskin in the fight for American independence. Of course, during the Civil War, many officers on both sides had horses that were famed far and wide. General Robert E. Lee's Traveler is probably the best known, but General Ulysses S. Grant had his Fox, and William T. Sherman had Duke. Some of these horses, by the way, were so beloved that they were buried close to their masters in a place of honor; Lee's Traveler was eventually buried beside him at Lee Chapel on the campus of Washington and Lee University. But it was not just the famous commanders of the war that had their favorite horses. So, too, did officers in the individual state regiments, and that's where our story, in a sense, ends, in Alton, New Hampshire's Riverside Cemetery. Here, you will find one nonhuman burial site for a locally famous warhorse named Old Tom.

The story of how Old Tom came to be buried here begins in 1862, when, in July, President Abraham Lincoln asked for 300,000 more men to fight for the Union cause in the Civil War. New Hampshire men immediately responded, raising a number of regiments. In Belknap County, on the southern shore of Lake Winnipesaukee, the Twelfth New Hampshire Infantry Regiment of volunteers had its beginning on July 25, 1862, when a meeting of prominent citizens from surrounding towns was convened at North Church in Laconia. Once the required state authorizations were obtained, enlistments began for the regiment on August 12, and within four days, enough men had joined to fill ten full companies. One of the officers of the newly formed Twelfth was Major George Savage (1818–1883) of Alton, who had previously served in the local militia and attained that same rank. An imposing man who stood six feet, two inches tall, Savage had since his youth had an interest in military affairs. He was born in neighboring New Durham and made his living as a farmer as a young man. In 1849, he moved to Alton and soon was involved in the shoemaking business and opened his own hotel, the Cocheco House. This historic hotel can still be seen today in the town's Monument Square Historic District, located in its northwest corner on Main Street, opposite its junction with Route 140. Savage was a major figure in the town's growth, being active in the Republican Party; a railroad commissioner beginning in 1851 for the Cocheco Railroad, whose construction began in 1848 and reached Alton by late 1851; and a state legislator in 1861–62. In fact, the first of the regiment's units, Company A, was recruited almost entirely by Savage, with his brother Moses Savage being elected captain. Once the company was organized in Alton, the men traveled to Concord, thereafter marching to the statehouse grounds with fife and drum playing martial music.

It is unclear just when Savage acquired Tom, likely a young beast, less than five years old, or where, but it was probably when the regiment first went off to war after its arrival in Washington, D.C., in late September or early October 1862. In general, horses provided to the army by its suppliers were inferior in quality compared to the horses of the South, but Savage's Tom would prove to be a fine horse. Interestingly, Tom was not the only famed horse to head off to war with the regiment; we also know that Sergeant Major Edwin Bedee of Meredith, a native of Sandwich, had his favorite mount, a horse named Clipper. He was so named not because of the speed typically associated with that name but because the horse had previously been owned in Maine but had his hair clipped by the man who sold him to Bedee after stealing him from his original owner. Once the theft was discovered, Bedee had to pay the rightful owner for the horse—being clipped of his money, so to speak, for a second time. So, the men and their steeds went off to war. Very soon, Savage and Tom made a name for themselves. Savage was known for being kind to his men and once told a fellow officer of the Twelfth, who was complaining about some of the men, "Don't be too severe. Remember we have the honor of commanding scores of men in this regiment, without as much as a corporal's stripe on their arms, who are better men than you or I dare be." Indeed, many a tired private in the Twelfth must have been happy to see their major come along astride Tom while on the march, "he often dismounting from his horse to give such one a ride or carry his knapsack. He possessed in an eminent degree those qualities of heart that served to endear

Portrait of Major George Savage of Alton. From Bartlett's *History of the Twelfth Regiment, New Hampshire Volunteers*, 1897.

him to the members of his regiment, and his memory is tenderly cherished by every surviving comrade."

Major George Savage's time in battle, like many Civil War soldiers, was destined to be rather short-lived, while Bedee saw a great amount of action, this capable man soon enough having gained a promotion to the rank of lieutenant in Company G. The men of the Twelfth went off to war and saw their first service, albeit in a limited role, at the Battle of Fredericksburg in December 1862. The following spring on May 2, 1863, the regiment experienced its first real battle action during the Battle of Chancellorsville. During that day, the Twelfth, as part of Whipple's Division in General Daniel Sickles's III Corps, was sent into action, opposing the Confederate troops of General Thomas "Stonewall" Jackson. The regiment played a rearguard action as night began to fall on May 2, covering the retreat of the battered Union XI Corps, and suffered a number of casualties. During that evening, with the sounds of Rebel soldiers not far off in the distance, the wounded men of the regiment, housed in an "old stable," were visited by the regiment's officers, including "Old Major" Savage, and urged to be quiet and sleep if they could. They were assured that they would be well guarded. The following day, May 3, the regiment was sent into battle, again in a rearward position, and was on the move that morning, with Major Savage astride Old Tom among the regimental officers leading the way. Early on, the Union commander saw that their position was untenable and ordered a retreat to re-form their lines. To cover this move, the Twelfth was among several regiments of their brigade sent forward into the woods to cover the move in the face of Stonewall Jackson's Virginians. The Twelfth was specifically ordered by Brigadier General Whipple to either hold the enemy in check "as long as possible" or "until the last man falls," depending on various accounts. Upon reaching their forward position, the situation was immediately a dire one, and within half an hour of the beginning of this firefight, one-third of the Twelfth New Hampshire's men were killed or wounded, with the officer cadre in particular suffering heavy casualties. The regiment's colonel and lieutenant colonel were both wounded and out of action, while Major Savage, shot through the jaw and severely wounded, was also out of action. His horse, Old Tom, was also wounded in the action but nonetheless was capable of staying on his feet and eventually reached safety, possibly with his bloodied master riding astride him. Many company captains were also wounded or killed in the action, among the latter being Captain Moses Savage, the major's brother. By the time the regiment withdrew from action, it did so under the command of a wounded Lieutenant Edwin Bedee astride his horse Clipper. During the two-hour fight, the Twelfth was largely fighting alone and unaware of what the rest of the Union army was doing, only knowing that they had retreated. When they finally reached the Union lines with Rebel soldiers not far off, the remnants of the regiment might have been shot down, taken for advancing Confederates, had not General Sickles, spotting their blue uniforms, told his men to hold their fire, crying out, "Those are my men in the front." When Lieutenant Bedee was asked, "What regiment, and where's the rest of it?" he replied, "Twelfth New Hampshire, and here's what's left of it." Indeed, the regiment had sustained the greatest number of Union casualties among all those engaged during the Battle of Chancellorsville, suffering 317 casualties among its 558 men, with 41 killed, 213 wounded and 63 captured. While the regiment was battered, it gained a reputation as a fighting unit, and with new recruits to replenish its ranks, it would see significant action later on during the heavy fighting at Gettysburg and Cold Harbor. As for Major Savage, his wounds largely ended his military career. Though he was promoted to lieutenant colonel for his action, other than briefly rejoining the regiment when it served at Point Lookout, Maryland, doing guard duty over a large Confederate prison camp, his fighting days were over. Upon his discharge from the army due to his wounds on May 28, 1864, Savage was given his horse and returned home, no doubt reaching Alton astride Old Tom.

As for Edwin Bedee and his horse Clipper, it would be a different story. Since Bedee was out of action for some time due to his wounds at Chancellorsville, he sold his warhorse to Major John Langley, who commanded the Twelfth at Gettysburg for a time. After his stint of command ended, Clipper was sold to Lieutenant Colonel Thomas Barker, who commanded the Twelfth longer than any other man. Clipper may have not been his original mount, but Barker was very proud of his warhorse and praised Clipper right up until the very end. In fact, it was during the fighting at Petersburg, Virginia, in July 1864, while the regiment was serving as a reserve, that Barker and his adjutant were observing the enemy's line while an artillery duel was being fought. It was just as Barker was standing by Clipper, telling his adjutant "about the superior merits of his charger" and "asked him if he didn't wish he had as good a one," when enemy fire struck the group. In the aftermath, the horse was "dead at the Colonel's feet, with a 12-pounder hole through his body." It was a sad end for such a noble beast but, alas, not an uncommon one. By some estimates, from one to three million horses and mules on all sides were killed during the war. No doubt, Clipper was probably left on the field and,

Photograph of Old Tom with his master, George Savage, in front of the well-known Cocheco House Hotel, from the grave site of Old Tom.

Old Tom's plot in Riverside Cemetery, Alton, the largest single burial plot in the entire cemetery.

perhaps, eventually buried in a large pit with others of his kind who were similarly killed. However, his fellow warhorse Tom would have a much different end.

After Major Savage, as he was locally known, returned home to Alton, he resumed his career as a hotel owner and even served as town sheriff for a few years. It's not hard to imagine Savage out and about performing his duties in company with Old Tom. It seemed likely that Savage would outlive his warhorse, but it was not to be. Savage died due to tuberculosis on February 17, 1883. Prior to this time, he had made known his wishes that his old warhorse be buried alongside him at Riverview Cemetery, but this was not possible, for town regulations forbade such a burial within its grounds. Thus, a space just outside the cemetery was procured and reserved for Old Tom, and when that venerable horse died in 1885, he was buried just outside the cemetery fence. Some years later, as the cemetery expanded in size, Old Tom was now in the confines of the cemetery, and there he lies to this day, his large grave site delineated by a wooden fence and marked with a small stone, as well as his picture, a very fitting tribute.

His master and companion, Major Savage, lies about 150 feet away. After old Tom's death, John Currier, Savage's son-in-law, penned a tribute to him. Here is a portion of that poem, which serves as a fine epitaph to the veteran warhorse of the Twelfth:

Old Tom is Dead!
As this is read
Though but a horse, how well his part he bore
'Midst shot and shell
And Rebel Yell;
'Midst cannon's roar
And scenes of gore
Unflinchingly he went! And who did more?

Old Tom is Dead!
How oft t'was said,
 "Here comes the Major and Old Tom";
How cheers arose as they passed on;
How proud he was, with step so high.
With head erect and flashing eye!
He seemed to know he was himself
A member of the brave old Twelfth.

Old Tom is Dead!
And thus t'was said
Of Major when, two years ago
He passed the picket-line of life.
Both now lie beyond all strife.
Both steed and rider gone; they rest,
Their honor bright, their memory blest.

CHAPTER II

A PLACE WHERE DEATH
IS JUST A NUMBER

During my career as an author and historian, I have visited hundreds of cemeteries in New Hampshire and beyond in New England over the years. These places, given their very nature, are thought provoking and offer moments for reflection. Many are also quite visually appealing, whether it be for their natural beauty, either landscaped or wild, or for the cemetery architecture found within, including elaborate monuments and delicate and fancy wrought-iron fencing. Then again, for many, it is all about the stories told on the stones themselves, of long-lived lives come to an end, of young lives tragically cut short or perhaps lifelong love or of young men who sacrificed their lives for our country. However, every once in a while, you find those places for the dead that offer none of these niceties, they instead being places of a much deeper, more somber reflection and of great mystery, causing us to wonder just who, really, is buried here. Such a place near Lake Winnipesaukee can be found on Old Granite Road (Route 171) in Ossipee Corner, not far from Courthouse Square and just minutes from Route 28, adjacent to the old Ossipee Town Cemetery. Here, on a sloping hillside on a barren patch of ground, will be found the final resting place for just over three hundred people, perhaps more. Most of the graves are simply marked with a small granite marker on which is carved one thing only: a number. This cemetery is known as the Carroll County Farm Cemetery or sometimes the Ossipee Pauper Cemetery. Locals have known of its existence all along and what its purpose was, but in modern times, until the last decade or so, it's been largely ignored or forgotten. Interest in the site was revived by local author M.J. Pettengill of North Sandwich, who did extensive historical research and recovered the names of many of those who are interred here, buried in local funeral home, state and county records. As a result of her herculean efforts, not only were the names of the dead brought to light, but a historical plaque was also erected on a granite boulder on the site in 2017. Pettengill wrote a historical novel, the first in an ongoing series, about the people of rural New Hampshire who are buried here, titled *Etched in Granite*. In fact, this forlorn place is a memorial to the people buried here and indicative of just how hard rural life in the late nineteenth and early twentieth centuries in the Lakes Region really was, despite all the tourist allure of the region. The cemetery is in fact a history lesson reminding us of just how difficult the lives of the most vulnerable people in society were in the days before Social Security and other social safety-net programs—the aged, the infirm, those with physical and mental handicaps, immigrants, single or widowed women and even veterans. It also, to this day, can be viewed as a cautionary tale about the ongoing plight of those who are the most vulnerable in our society, especially in rural areas.

View of the Carroll County Farm Cemetery in Ossipee.

In the days before state and federal social programs, the poor were provided for as best as was possible at the town level—each community responsible for its own. Early on, the poor, infirm and elderly who could not care for themselves were actually put up for bid by the town, a kind of foster care system, where those willing to take these folks in were paid a yearly stipend by the town to cover expenses. The level of care surely varied from household to household; some of the vulnerable were either overworked, neglected or abused, but many others were well cared for. Either way, there was no formal system in place to manage this vulnerable population. However, as the times and attitudes changed in New Hampshire and beyond, and with many communities growing in size, by the mid-nineteenth century, towns big and small began to establish poor farms. These establishments offered dormitory-style housing (where lack of privacy was the norm) and food for the inmates committed there, again because of old age, chronic health issues or their lack of means to support themselves. Those who resided at these poor farms were also expected, if physically capable, to work on the poor farm itself, helping to cultivate and grow crops for both the inmates and, if possible, surplus that could be sold at a profit, as well as perform other manual labor and maintenance chores. In short, life was not easy on these poor farms, but they did at least provide a modicum of care. Many of the inmates, especially the aged and handicapped, were forced to come here because they either had no surviving family members to care for them or those families were unable or unwilling to do so. In some cases, young, unwed pregnant mothers were housed here, perhaps kicked out of their homes, while sometimes young men who were transient laborers also ended up in these establishments at times when they were unable to find work. These poor farms, which were mostly organized on a county basis, were once quite extensive, and wherever you see the commonly named "Poor Farm Road" anywhere in the state, it's a sure sign of where such an institution was once located. As for the Carroll County Farm, it was located in Ossipee on what is now County Farm Road off Route 171, several miles or so to the west of the cemetery on land now occupied by the Mountain View Nursing Home and the Carroll County Superior Court, as well as the house of corrections.

Pauper cemeteries like this are not uncommon in New England, but you have to search hard to find them, as many have been lost over the years due to neglect or deliberate development. Most times, while the names of the dead were recorded in county records, burials either went unmarked altogether or, if a marker was provided, it provided the barest of information. The numbering system such as was used here was not an uncommon one used in New England (even by the Shaker religious sect), the idea being that, if someone truly wished to know the identity of the individual—which seemed most unlikely given that these individuals on the poor farm often had no family—the number given would correspond to data written down in an ongoing record book. In rare cases, as with the Shakers, these records were meticulously kept and preserved, but for many poor farms, these records were lost at a later date, scattered in various files or only haphazardly kept in the first place. After all, these dead were from the lowest rungs on the ladder of society, and just as their regular lives were passed in obscurity, so, too, should it not be surprising that the preservation of their identities after death was not taken so seriously.

So, regarding the inhabitants of this cemetery, just who is buried here? Well, the names and numbers rescued by Pettengill tell an interesting, albeit sad, story. Of the approximately 310 graves here today, about 56 are of those whose identities are unknown, while of the remainder, 148 are men, 102 are women and 4 are infants or children. The adults who are buried here died due to a variety of factors. "Old age" was a common death designation, but heart disease, kidney (Bright's) disease, dementia, tuberculosis, influenza and meningitis are also found in the records. There can be no doubt that some deaths were due to communicable diseases that spread within the poor farm itself. Young Bertha Morrison O'Hare, buried at marker #240, died on October 21, 1918, from pneumonia brought on by influenza. Given the date of her death, one can't help but wonder if she died of the Spanish flu pandemic. She was born in Bridgeton, Maine, and was living in Chatham, New Hampshire, before coming here. One also can't help but wonder how she came to be at the poor farm in the first place. She arrived there at the age of twenty-three in 1904 and remained there for the last fourteen years of her life. Did she have physical or developmental needs that forced her family to place her there? I doubt we can ever know her full story. As for the ages of the dead, while some infants and children are buried here, the vast majority were in their mid-fifties or older when they died. Some undoubtedly had ongoing health issues, but others were simply older folks who had no one to care for them and nowhere else to go, likely unable to live on their own any longer. The listed occupations for the deceased also paint a picture. Most of the women are listed as "housewives" or domestic workers, while the men were "laborers" and one man was listed as teamster. The poor farm was seldom a place where professional men, like doctors and lawyers, spent the last years of their lives. Several veterans at least are buried here as well, with no flags or emblems to mark their forgotten graves on Memorial Day.

Grave marker #194, Carroll County Farm Cemetery, the burial site of Frank Wilkinson, 1907.

Research shows that John Hubbard of Wakefield (grave #111) and Andrew Wentworth of Wolfeboro (grave #180) both served in the Thirteenth New Hampshire Regiment during the Civil War, seeing action, among other places, at the Battle of Cold Harbor. Meanwhile, Franklin Wilkinson of Freedom (grave #194) served in the First Regiment New Hampshire Volunteer Heavy Artillery and was mustered out of service in Washington, D.C., in 1865 before returning home to a hard life.

While most of those buried here were born in New Hampshire or neighboring Maine, at least eighteen of them were immigrants who came here from Canada (ten in number), Ireland (four), England (three) and Scotland (one). The first immigrant known to be buried here, Ann Conley of Ireland (grave #29), died in 1873, while the last known immigrant buried here was Amelia McCloud (grave #278), who died in 1930 and was from Canada. We can't help but wonder about the life journeys that brought them here. Among the infants buried here is Archie Quimby (grave #145), who died of meningitis at age two in 1897. He was born at the Carroll County Farm to his parents, George and Ellen Quimby, which illustrates the fact that many married couples in dire straits also lived here. While for those known children graves, several names are known (including babies Bagley and Tibbetts, grave numbers #119 and #120 in 1890), grave #198 is for a baby who died in 1907 whose name was either unrecorded or forgotten. Such is the fate of the youngest of the poor in an earlier time. And, of course, there were the elderly couples who spent their last days at the poor farm, including Lafayette Hanson (died March 1938) and his wife, Lettie (died December 1939), he a mill hand, she a dressmaker, both buried in unmarked graves, as well as James Carter (grave #215), died March 1912, and his wife, Emma Harriman Carter (grave #259), who died in January 1925.

All of this uncovered information about these individuals buried here from about 1870 into the 1950s (with the site apparently still used on rare occasions to this day) does reveal something about the harder side of life in the region, and while the dead from the Carroll County Farm were given just a number to mark their final resting place, it also reminds us that they were people who, in the end, were probably not so different than we are today.

CHAPTER 12

THE GREAT WALL OF SANDWICH

We've all seen them. Wherever you travel in New Hampshire and New England, especially in the more rural areas, stone walls aren't hard to come by. A ubiquitous part of the landscape, they can be seen in fields and meadows, along rural and heavily traveled roads and off the beaten path, deep in the woods in places long since overgrown. Seldom do we think, how did they come to be here? Who built them, and why? In fact, most of the traditional stone walls you see in New Hampshire date from the great craze for sheep farming that began in the early 1800s when Merino sheep were first imported to this country in New England. Like the rest of the region, New Hampshire farmers took to sheep farming, clearing thousands of acres of land and keeping their flocks contained by fencing off their land with stone walls, building countless miles' worth in aggregate. By the 1840s, there were more than two sheep in New Hampshire for every one human being, about 600,000 in all. However, not all stone walls are equal, and not all of them were built for the same purpose, and that's where our next featured site comes into the picture. In your travels around the Lakes Region, don't forget to pay the historic town of Sandwich a visit. Lying between and betwixt the Lakes Region and the White Mountains Region, it has much to offer in the way of natural beauty and historic architecture. One of the most fascinating examples of the town's man-made structures is the so-called Great Wall of Sandwich, which can be found as you travel from the Lower Historic District on Wentworth Hill Road (Route 109) down Little Pond Road. Just a short way from their junction, you will see a large stone wall that runs for perhaps a half mile on the left-hand side of the road. However, this is no ordinary stone wall, nor is it a modern one. It was actually built in 1874–75 by master masons Jacob Roberts of East Sandwich and his assistant, Curt Prime of Moultonborough. The wall, which comprises several sections, including one running at a right angle from the main portion, is over a mile in length and in some places ten feet wide and is about four feet tall. A close-up inspection will reveal that this is not just a single wall but actually a double stone wall, with a massive amount of rocks filling the interior space between the two walls.

No wall this massive and well constructed was ever built just to contain a herd of sheep, and neither was this was one. Commissioned by Isaac Adams, it was merely built on a grand scale to delineate his landed estate. The Great Wall of Sandwich is made even more notable by a larger-than-life statue of the Greek goddess Niobe that stands on a pedestal at the top of a massive cut-granite ledge, complete with steps, which serves as both the focal and starting point of the Great Wall as it extends down the hill with a view of the Ossipee Mountains in the background. A rock wall is one thing, but one adorned with a mythological statue is another. How this stone wall came to be built in all its glory starts with a man named Isaac Adams. For certain, he was a mechanical genius and an inventor of great importance, but he also seems to have had an unlikable personality and was perhaps a bit paranoid and vindictive. Our story starts in Sandwich in 1820, when Isaac Adams (1802–1883) arrived here from his native town of Rochester, New Hampshire, to serve as an apprentice to cabinetmaker Benjamin Jewett. Due to the death of his father when he was just nine years old, life was not always easy for Adams. He worked at a cotton mill in Dover for several years at the age of ten or eleven and then worked in a cabinet shop before coming to Sandwich. However, he was treated well by the Jewett family and liked his time here, so much so that he encouraged his brother Seth Adams to apprentice here beginning in 1821.

In 1824, Isaac Adams decided to make a move to the big city of Boston to find his fortune and asked some of Jewett's neighbors, Colonel Joseph Wentworth and William Weed (both rich and prominent men in town), for the money to pay his coach fare for the trip. The loan was refused, however, with local legend stating that the men thought that Adams wouldn't amount to much or was a ne'er-do-well and that they'd never see their money again. Adams is said to have replied in angry fashion, "I can work my way to Boston, and I shall do so, and when I come back, I will be able to purchase your farm, if not all the farms in Sandwich."

Well, Isaac Adams did indeed make his way down to Boston and at first worked in a machine shop, never taking up the trade of cabinetmaker. Adams also had a fertile mind and started the invention of his Adams Power Press by 1827, with the new style of printing press introduced three years later. In less than a decade, by 1836, the Adams Power Press had taken the world by storm. It not only revolutionized the printing industry in America, but his presses were sold worldwide, and book publishing was never the same again. The press reduced the cost of printing a book substantially and became the dominant printing press used for the rest of the century in America. Needless to say, Isaac Adams earned a fortune and was a wealthy man the remainder of his life. He formed the I. and S. Adams Company

Portrait of Sandwich resident and printing press inventor Isaac Adams. From Thomas Simonds's *History of South Boston*, 1857.

with his brother Seth (who was previously noted for the sugar refinery he operated in the Boston area) and not only sold his printing press but was active in Massachusetts politics as a state senator for a brief time, as well as being involved in the Massachusetts Emigrant Aid Company, which was formed to transport antislavery immigrants to the new Kansas Territory in the hopes of making Kansas a free state.

Though Adams had many activities going on in Massachusetts, he retained a fondness for Sandwich, sending his son Isaac Jr. to the Sandwich Academy for schooling, where he boarded with his old master and friend Benjamin Jewett. Upon his retirement from active business after selling his patent rights and turning his business over to a son, Isaac Adams made the decision to move back to Sandwich by 1861 and was again a full-time resident of the town in which he had been an apprentice fifty years before. He also held true to his word by buying up many adjoining properties in town, starting with land he first acquired in 1855 and later including the land once owned by Joseph Wentworth (who was long dead), who had refused a simple loan to a young lad trying to make his way in the world. As Sandwich historian Patricia Heard has written, acquiring these parcels of land "had an almost spiritual significance for him." In all, Isaac Adams would come to own some 2,600 acres of land between Red Hill Pond and Little's Pond, his personal estate being an elaborate one with a windmill, a duck pond, flower gardens, grape arbors and "sleek cattle" that "ranged the fields." Of course, enclosing a portion of it was the Great Wall of Sandwich, as it was later known. Adams had originally planned to enclose his entire estate within a wall, but only this section was ever built. Many modern-day accounts refer to the Great Wall as a kind of "spite fence" on a grand scale, but its beautiful design and height in general (less than ten feet) takes it out of this category. Now, Adams certainly had an "I'll show them" attitude on his mind when he returned to Sandwich, but he treated most people in town fairly, especially those who worked for him, and was said to have paid "generously" for the land he acquired and more than fair wages to his workers, including the one hundred men who worked on the wall for a year. The wall itself is an engineering marvel, and Adams probably helped design some of its features, including parts of the wall that collected rainwater and channeled it into underground pipes that drain outside the wall, as well as into underground wells. The width of the wall also has led to the legend that Adams drove his coach on top of the wall around his estate, but the several deliberate breaks in the wall and its method of construction discount this idea entirely. The rock for the wall was gathered from several different sources, including the foundations of homes on the lots that Adams had demolished, from the land on which the wall itself was built and from several quarries located a short distance away. While much of the land within the wall is wooded today, it was once open land and fields, offering a clear view into the distance. By the early part of this century, however, much of the Great Wall was overgrown until the wall was repaired and the natural growth removed in 2004–09 to preserve and make it more visible as in the days of old.

The Great Wall of Sandwich, however, would not be as great without the magnificent statue that overlooks what has now been long referred to as "Image Hill." The statue of the Greek goddess Niobe, which is made of zinc and painted white, was likely cast by German sculptor Moritz Geiss in Berlin, Germany, circa 1860. Geiss was one of the pioneers in developing the use of the metal for statue-making. Based on a copy of an ancient original, the statue of Niobe was advertised for sale at the London Industrial Exposition in 1862 by Geiss, along with two other statues. All were purchased by an anonymous buyer, thought to be Isaac Adams since he was traveling in Europe at the time and, by later accounts, was said to have bought his statues there. Once the Great Wall was finished, the statue of Niobe was placed there, originally standing on a twenty-foot-tall pedestal, a true work of art in a rural New Hampshire community that, perhaps not coincidentally, would

The Great Wall of Sandwich looking eastward. The land within its walls was once cleared but has now reverted to forest.

soon gain the renown as an artists' colony that it retains to this day. Niobe stood in her original spot from 1875 to 1941, when the combination of a hurricane and a weakened pedestal brought her down. Isaac Adams never stated why he chose that statue in particular; undoubtedly, he had a love of classical antiquities (one of the other statues he purchased, that of the goddess Diana, was displayed on his estate until its eventual sale in 2010), but is there more to the story? Local scholars believe that Niobe, "punished by the gods for her hubris," was a deliberate choice by Adams for the lessons it symbolized regarding his treatment at the hands of town elders all those years ago. While it's not hard to believe this theory, that the statue is "itself an emblem of his power and wealth, to constantly remind townsfolk" of what Isaac Adams had become is most certainly evident.

After the statue's fall, its shattered pieces of zinc, some large and some very small, were gathered and eventually ended up under a manure pile in an old barn on the estate, whose land was broken up and sold in parcels in the years after Adams's death. These pieces were rediscovered in 2004 and were eventually put back together by metal artisan and Sandwich resident

The restored statue of the Greek goddess Niobe, which stands at the head of the Great Wall of Sandwich.

Adam Nudd-Homeyer beginning in 2011 during a painstaking and exacting restoration process that was also a labor of love. Niobe has now reclaimed her rightful spot on Image Hill, much to the joy of locals and visitors alike. The home located adjacent to the statue of Niobe is also a historic one, despite its modern appearance. The structure, known as Adams Hall, was originally built in 1848 and was first located on Wentworth Hill Road near its junction with School House Road. It had a dance hall on the second floor and four artisan shops on the ground floor. The building was later purchased by Isaac Adams, possibly one of his earliest land acquisitions in Sandwich, and moved to its current site by him in 1875. It is likely that he resided here on a temporary basis until his larger home was built farther up the hill, the building offering him a nice view of his statue and Great Wall, as well as of the mountains in the distance, as it does for its current owners.

The strange and temperamental genius who was Isaac Adams, whose land and private holdings were valued at $565,000 in the 1880 federal census (equal to $15 million in 2020 dollars), would not live out the remainder of his days in country solitude. He got involved in town government as a selectman and several other posts and quite often was contentious with his neighbors and rivals. He also was not afraid to litigate against those he felt had wronged him or the town, and his personal life was a mess. He often argued with his second wife, Anna, and when she left him for a time, he even won a suit against the stagecoach driver who had carried his wife and her belongings (which he claimed as his) away. He and his wife, in fact, frequently fought in public, the *New York Times* even reporting that he had fired his pistol and was noted for his eccentricities, including running around outside in his shirt. He also at one point fired his gun against his neighbor's "damned dogs." There are many more details like this in the remaining years of Isaac Adams's life that make us question his faculties, and even after his death, his will, whose amount was valued somewhere between $2 and 3 million, was contested by his son Julius, a fierce protector of his mother, "on the ground of mental incapacity." One final note about the Adams family: it is curious, perhaps, that Isaac's beloved brother Seth, who also became a wealthy man, upon his death bequeathed $600,000 for the establishment of the Adams Nervine Asylum in Jamaica Plain, Massachusetts, in 1877 for the treatment of the indigent who were not insane but "debilitated" and "nervous," conditions perhaps he had watched his brother deal with his whole life. In the end, it is hard to believe now, as one takes a drive down quiet Little Pond Road in the Image Hill area, that such hubris was taking place, but the wall, at least in part, is a reminder that such was the case.

CHAPTER 13

THE HIDDEN LIVES
OF AFRICAN AMERICANS

Anyone who has spent any time in New Hampshire, whether visitor or lifelong resident, knows that the Granite State is not an ethnically diverse place, especially the farther north you travel. Percentage-wise, the state's population of those identified as African American or Black has typically hovered around two-tenths of 1 percent, though in 1790, the first year of the federal census, it came in at six-tenths of 1 percent. The state's population would not break this barrier until the year 2000, and as of the 2010 census, it sits at 1.1 percent. In terms of sheer numbers, well under one thousand African Americans lived in the state in any given census until the year 1960. So, there you have it; New Hampshire is a largely white state, and beyond our so-called urban areas to the south and on the seacoast, that number in the Lakes Region is even lower. The Belknap County towns located on the south shore of Lake Winnipesaukee discussed herein averaged just twenty-one residents of color in aggregate in the census counts from 1860 to 1940, while the Carroll County towns on the north shore of the lake averaged less than half this amount, the lowest of any county in the state. These low numbers make for a hidden presence of sort for African Americans throughout the area's history, and individuals are often difficult to fully identify, but with the help of census and military records, some information is to be gained. While the tangible evidence for African Americans in the area is often lacking outside of official records and a few gravestones in local cemeteries, their story, such as it can be told, is nonetheless a fascinating one that deserves attention, for their lives had meaning, and they, too, made contributions to the society at large. Among the twenty or so families discussed below, some fought for our country's independence in the American Revolution, while many others fought for a different kind of freedom in the Civil War. Their lives are worthy of remembrance on this account alone.

In regard to some of the general life details of African Americans in the Lakes Region, most of the men were employed as farmhands, while those who were slightly better off financially either rented their own farmland or owned a small plot of farmland. Those who were farmhands often worked in a variety of towns over the course of their working years and moved from town to town. Those who worked in the larger city of Laconia were sometimes employed as truckmen or teamsters or worked in factory jobs or in the railroad industry. As for the women, many helped to tend the family farm in addition to their domestic duties of managing the household and child-rearing. However, others were employed as domestic help in local white households, while some in the larger towns like Laconia were employed in the mills or as seamstresses, dressmakers and laundresses or cooks in local establishments. In both cases, whether man or woman, the jobs they worked were tough manual labor occupations that usually involved long working hours for wages that were low on the economic scale. As to family relations, the information below will show that in places where multiple African American families lived, the bonds between these families were very strong, no doubt due to both their color and shared experiences. Intermarrying between these families was also quite common. Indeed, it is quite clear that these families usually helped and looked after one another. Despite this, young free Black men did sometimes marry outside their community, and mixed-race marriages between them and white females in this area of rural New Hampshire were also common. Was there a social stigma attached to these marriages on the part of both Blacks and whites alike? Almost certainly there was in society at large, but on the local level, this was much less of an issue. This may be due in part to the fact that many of the white women in these marriages came from farming families that were often on a similar economic level as that of the Black families. It is also likely true that in most cases, local farmers would have known of these young Black farmers and farmhands firsthand and knew them to be good men and hard workers who could provide for their daughters who were in love with them. Finally, as to schooling, many of the children from these Black families attended the local village schools and were given an equal opportunity in regard to public education. Indeed, as historian Warren Clarke has documented in his excellent study for the town of Gilmanton, many of these children were mentioned frequently in school reports for their perfect attendance.

Our first glimpse of African American lives in the area comes under the unfortunate guise of slavery…yes, there were slaves held in this area, though the numbers were small. Wolfeboro was possibly the first town to see the practice of slavery when Royal Governor John Wentworth built his summer estate here beginning in 1768 (see chapter 2). During the several years that his land was cleared, some of this work may have been performed by Wentworth's personal slaves, and after he and Lady Wentworth were finally able to enjoy their summer home beginning in 1770, they were also likely attended to by slaves who accompanied them on the journey from Portsmouth. In the spring of 1775, with the advent of the American Revolution, Wentworth left Wolfeboro in haste, never to return. Left on his land was a slave family that included a woman named Hagar (a typical slave name based on an African woman in the book of Genesis in the Bible who was also a slave), her young son and her husband. Within a short time, Hagar's husband was killed while cutting down trees on the Wentworth estate. In the aftermath of this tragic event, the "widow's mind became deranged and she took her little son and wandered away, ending her rambles in New Durham, where they were taken in by the family of Samuel Willey," according to town historian Ellen Jennings. We know not exactly in what year this event took place, probably sometime in 1775, nor do we know anything of Hagar's travels and how she came to end up in New Durham. Was she given food and temporary shelter along the way by sympathetic white families, or did she just scrape by on her own? And why did New Durham become her final destination? Was it by mere chance, or did she go there with a purpose? In the end, we can never know, but the sorrow and despair that drove her on her journey isn't hard to imagine. Once Hagar made New Durham, she largely disappears, and the remainder of her life story is unknown. However, her son, who subsequently went by the name of Remus Willey, stayed in town and "lived all his long life in this town."

Remus was probably the only Black person in New Durham at that time, but if so, it would not be for long. In 1783, Colonel Thomas Tash, formerly of Newmarket, New Hampshire, arrived here with his wife, taking up residence on the eastern side of Bay Road. It has been written by town historian Ellen Jennings that Tash "and his lady lived in grand style…and they had several slaves to do all the work." Once again, the names of the slaves are not known for certain, but they were likely Oxford Tash, the colonel's longtime slave, and possibly his wife, Esther How Freeman Tash, who was not a slave at all. Oxford Tash was a veteran of the American Revolution, fighting for both New Hampshire and Massachusetts beginning in late 1775, seeing action for New Hampshire at Fort Ticonderoga and probably in his master's own militia regiment at the Battle of White Plains and later on in the Eleventh Massachusetts Continental Regiment at the Battles of Saratoga and Monmouth. During his time in service, he not only survived a bout of smallpox but also was wounded in action "and carried the musket ball then received in his thigh until his death." Tash later served at West Point and was present at the hanging of the famed British spy John André before his eventual discharge in February 1781. He married his wife, Esther, in Newburyport, Massachusetts, in November 1781 before returning home to Colonel Tash. Whether Oxford was given his freedom immediately as a result of his war service is uncertain, but I suspect he helped his master Thomas Tash one final time in his move to New Durham before parting ways with him and returning to the seacoast to live in Exeter with Esther. The couple's first child was born there in March 1784. By the time of the 1790 census, there were no people of color living in New Durham. The subsequent whereabouts of Remus Willey, despite claims of a "long life" in town, are unknown, though it seems likely that a son or grandson of his, Silas Willey, age fourteen and working as a farmhand, was residing in Gilmanton in 1860.

The town of Alton, too, was home to a veteran of the American Revolution. Peleg Runnals was a slave in Rhode Island when he enlisted in the First Rhode Island Regiment in early 1778, with the promise that after two years of service he would be a free man. After serving in the Battle of Rhode Island and other garrison duty, Runnals was indeed discharged as a free man and first made his way north to Salem, Massachusetts, where he married his wife, Martha Hall, in 1778. The couple subsequently moved farther north into New Hampshire, living in Somersworth and then Rochester before finally making their home in Alton. Among the couple's many children was Jack Runnals, who in 1790 had a household that included five other people, likely including his mother and father. Peleg Runnals died in Alton in September 1832, but no gravestone marks this veteran's final resting place. It is interesting to note that Alton also had two other free Blacks living in town in 1790, both quite possibly members of the Runnals family, who were likely working as servants for Joseph Pierce and Benjamin Bennett.

In several other towns, African Americans both free and enslaved are also found in early records. In Moultonborough, Duncan McNaughton, a former British soldier who lived to the incredible age of 115 before his death in 1831, had in his household one slave, name unknown, in 1790. Likely this man was freed long before McNaughton's death, though it must be pointed out that slavery was not officially abolished in New Hampshire until after the end of the Civil War with the ratification of the Thirteenth Amendment in 1865. In Meredith, a free Black by the name of Peter Moulton was counted in the 1790 census, his household having four other persons of color, as well as one white female who may have been his wife. Though it is uncertain, he was likely the former slave of Benning Moulton, who arrived in neighboring Center Harbor in 1783. He was the son of Colonel Jonathan Moulton, the original grantee and founder of Moultonborough and New Hampton. Colonel Moulton was a slaveholder, and it is likely that his son, too, had a slave or two who accompanied him from his hometown of Hampton to Center Harbor.

While the numbers in other Lake Winnipesaukee towns have always been small, the largest population of African Americans in the area for many years was found in Gilmanton, which in colonial times was one of the largest towns in the state and included land that was later set off as the towns of Belmont and Gilford. "Gilmantown," as it was once known, counted a population of just four African Americans, all slaves, in the special census of 1775 at the beginning of the American Revolution. However, fifteen years after the war ended, the first census of 1790 showed twenty-three people of color living there. Only one of these individuals was listed as a slave, he being Prince Cogswell, owned by Jeremy Cogswell. Five other free Blacks, names and genders unknown, are also listed in the households of white citizens, two in the household of Thomas Cogswell and one each in the households of Peaslee Badger, Samuel Jewett Jr. and Joseph Jones. All these men were prominent in town, and it is highly likely that the free Blacks living with them were employed as servants or hired hands. It is possible that most of them had once been slaves, perhaps freed after the war, but it is also possible that they were still slaves, even if not listed as such by the census. Indeed, for that 1790 census, anecdotal information from the time suggests that in New England, de facto slaves—individuals once purchased and with no other home or income and holdings of any kind—were reported as being "free" for the census because of the recognized incongruity of holding people in bondage after we had just fought our own War of Independence against the British and the recent establishment of the Constitution as the law of the land (by New Hampshire's ratification) in 1788.

While we can never know the true status of these five individuals, the census does tell us that there were also four free Black families who lived in town, composing the largest category of African Americans. Three of these heads of Black households—Cato Wallingford, Caesar Wallis (Wallace) and Robinson Peters—were Revolutionary War soldiers. Wallingford, who came to town with his wife, Pegg, was formerly the slave of Colonel Thomas Wallingford of Somersworth and gained his freedom by serving in the war. He joined the Second New Hampshire Regiment in March 1777 and fought at the Battles of Hubbardston, Saratoga and Monmouth during his three years of service. After the war, he first lived in Exeter but was forced to leave that town, "warned out" because of his low economic status, and came to Gilmanton. His stay here was not a long one. He returned to the Exeter area, where he disappears from the records by 1799. Caesar Wallis was also a former slave, but his origin is uncertain. He first saw service in the Revolutionary War probably for Massachusetts and later with New Hampshire's Second Continental Regiment, seeing action at the Battles of Bunker Hill, Oriskany and Monmouth. Indeed, he saw extensive service from 1775 until his final discharge in 1783, having served for five years overall, longer than most men, white or Black. In fact, at his discharge, he was given a Badge of Merit certificate signed personally by General George Washington attesting to his long and faithful service. Before his service ended, Wallis married Katie Duce of Exeter, and sometime after his discharge, they moved to Gilmanton. He would live in the Lakes Region the remainder of his life. The couple had one known child, Lucy, and would later, at an unknown date, move to neighboring Meredith for a time until later moving back to Gilmanton in about 1821. He and his wife were cared for in their old age by John Page. The date of Caesar Wallis's death is unknown, but it was likely sometime around April 1827, as his last pension payment for his war service was the previous month. He is said to have been buried on the Piper family farm above Meredith Center in an unmarked grave with other members of his family. A final Black Revolutionary War soldier then living in Gilmanton was Robinson Peters, whose household had seven members in 1790. He was likely enslaved in Newmarket prior to the war, but this is not certain, and he began his military service in 1777 at the age of twenty-five. He saw brief duty as a militiaman and later served as a sailor in the Massachusetts State Navy aboard the eighteen-gun brig *Vengeance*, which was destroyed during the ill-fated Penobscot Expedition, when he and the rest of the crew took to the woods and made their way back to New Hampshire. His war service over, Peters returned to the seacoast area, where he married a woman named Violet in Exeter in September 1781. He and his family were living in Gilmanton by 1790 but would move by 1792 to Meredith, where he was still a resident in 1832, when he finally received a pension for his wartime service. The question may be asked, why did these men move here? Since all came from the more populous seacoast area and were once enslaved, it is most likely they came here for one or more of several reasons. First, land was available here at a cheaper rate than on the coast for these men trying to establish a new life of freedom. Secondly, after the war, it was not unheard of for free Blacks in southern New Hampshire and Massachusetts to be kidnapped and sold into slavery in the South. The possibility of this happening farther north in New Hampshire, where the Black population was small and nefarious slave traders would have stuck out like a sore thumb, was almost zero. Finally, it seems that Gilmanton, perhaps for the reasons just stated, became a mecca for free Blacks. With one family established in town, this probably served to attract subsequent Black families as they were looking for a new home and neighbors of color that they could socialize with. In fact, because these families grouped together over the years, one section of town had a "N****r Road" and a "N***** Hill," names given by the whites in Gilmanton to the area where African Americans lived in the southwest part of town along Province and Meadow Pond Roads. Thankfully, this bit of racial ugliness vanished from the local vocabulary long ago.

The African American presence in Gilmanton would remain strong for over one hundred years as other Black families also moved to town in the mid-nineteenth century. Probably the most prominent Black family was that of John Battis. He originally came from Canterbury, New Hampshire, the son of Samuel Battis, where his descendants included his probable grandfather Sampson Battis (aka Sampson Moore, once enslaved by Colonel Archaelus Moore of Concord), a veteran of the American Revolution, as well as his probable great-grandfather John Battis, who was a veteran of the French and Indian War of the 1750s and 1760s. John Battis of Gilmanton was born in 1831 and came here after the Civil War, in which he served in the Sixth New Hampshire Regiment, to become a farmer. His farm was smaller than that of most whites but was enough to support his wife, Lydia (born circa 1830); daughters Lorrin (who worked on the family farm at age fourteen in 1870), Emma (born circa 1862) and Kelvina (born circa 1871); and sons John (born circa 1873), Walter (born circa 1875) and Harry (born circa 1877). His life was certainly more difficult after the death of his wife in the late 1870s, but he seemed to prevail and was likely a leader in the small Black community until his death in 1912. His son John Henry Battis remained in the area for years, but by the time he married Sadie Veasey in September 1895, he was considered a white man. The Battis name remained a common one in town well into the mid-twentieth century. Calvin Battis, John's brother, would also come from Canterbury to Gilmanton by 1870, his household including his wife, Ann (born circa 1832), daughter Martha (born circa 1863) and a young Black girl, Olive Moody (born circa 1862), who was boarding with the family while attending school in 1870. One family among many that had close ties to the Battis family were the Haskells, who also originated in Canterbury. Among them was Charles C. Haskell (born January 1838). His father was Ephraim Haskell and his mother Elza Battis. As a young man, he worked as a farm laborer and married his wife, Laura Perry Haskell, a white woman from Hopkinton employed as a housekeeper, on December 7, 1862. Just over a year later, on December 10, 1863, Charles Haskell enlisted in the Eleventh United States Colored Heavy Artillery Regiment for service in the Civil War and was stationed in the area around New Orleans, seeing limited action. Upon being mustered out of service on October 2, 1865, Charles and Laura lived in Concord for a time, but by 1880, they were living in Belmont. Charles was employed as a farm laborer after the war and after Laura's death in 1896. He would subsequently work in several towns where he was counted in census records, including Gilford (1890), Tilton (1900) and lastly Laconia, where he died in September 1924. Both he and his wife are buried in Laconia's Union Cemetery.

Among Gilmanton's other notable Black residents by 1880 were Nathaniel Robinson, Elijah Hale, Alonzo Burbank, William Sydney, Moses Dustin and George Cogswell, all but one of whom were Civil War veterans. Nathaniel Robinson was probably of mixed heritage, described as being "black" in the 1870 census and "mulatto" in the 1880 census. He was a farm worker who supported his wife, Mary, who was white and whose occupation was described as "keeping house." The couple had four children, Annie, Cora, Lola (all described as "mulatto") and an infant named Mary (described as "white"). He was also born in Canterbury but, most interestingly, hired a substitute to serve in his place during the Civil War, quite possibly because he had just married in November 1860 and had a large family to support.

Elijah Hale is also an interesting man. He was born in Mississippi about 1841 and was residing in Newton, Massachusetts, by the time of the Civil War, enlisting in the all-Black Fifth Massachusetts Cavalry on March 26, 1864, and serving through October 1865. He made his way to Gilmanton by 1880 (probably much earlier) for the reason that his wife was from Meredith, she being the daughter of Lucy Wallace, the daughter of Revolutionary War soldier Caesar Wallace. Here Hale lived with his wife and their son

The gravestone of Civil War veteran Charles C. Haskell, Union Cemetery, Laconia.

Willie. Given his birth in the Deep South, it is highly possible that Hale had previously been a slave, perhaps one who escaped to the North via the Underground Railroad. He died in Gilmanton in September 1888 due to Bright's disease, but his widow remained in the area, living in Gilford by 1890 and dying in Laconia on February 20, 1917.

Alonzo Burbank was another Civil War veteran who settled in Gilmanton and whose family would have a presence here for nearly one hundred years. A native of Hopkinton, New Hampshire, he joined the New Hampshire Battalion of the First Regiment of New England Voluntary Cavalry (First Regiment Rhode Island Cavalry) at the age of twenty-three on January 11, 1862, and soon headed off to war. Serving in Company L, Burbank was among the members of the troop that were captured in the Battle of Middleburg in Virginia on June 18, 1863. Burbank was later that year paroled and returned to his regiment. Gaining the rank of corporal, his service ended at Winchester, Virginia, on January 22, 1865, after which he returned home. He married his wife, Lucia Dustin (from another well-known Black family in the area), of Concord in 1867 and by 1880 was a resident of Gilmanton. Like John Battis, Alonzo Burbank was likely of mixed heritage and perhaps light-skinned, as he was classified as being white in the 1880 census and Black in the 1900 census. He was employed as a farmhand and must have been a hardworking man, for he had a large family to support, including his daughters Addie, Bertha and Charlotte (all considered "mulatto"), as well as his oldest daughter, Nellie (classified as white). In 1880, he also had seventeen-year-old Mattie Battis as a boarder while she was attending school in Gilmanton. Another child, namesake Alonzo (often called "Lonnie"), was born in 1890. He would marry in Gilmanton in 1910 and in turn have a son named Alonzo, who died in 1977.

William Sidney, born circa 1835, was a native of the West Indies whose racial designation changed over the years in the census. A resident of Goffstown, he enlisted in the Second New Hampshire Regiment on August 7, 1861, and was severely wounded in the Second Battle of Bull Run in August 1862. Once he recovered, he rejoined his regiment, and his service ended at Petersburg, Virginia, on August 24, 1864. He returned to New Hampshire and first lived in Meredith, but by 1880, he was residing in Gilmanton with his young wife, Sarah (born circa 1862). He was employed as a farmhand and identified as a mulatto. By 1910, he was living in nearby Belmont and was first listed as being white; the records were subsequently written over and changed to a designation of Black. What became of this family after this time is uncertain.

Moses Dustin is a man whose name, perhaps, is the best known of Gilmanton's Black veterans, not for his life, but for his burial site. When he died on January 28, 1895, in Gilmanton, he was interred in Beech Grove Cemetery, in a spot that was then just outside the cemetery walls. Two different tales are told as to why this location was chosen; the first states that the people in town didn't want to be near him when he was alive and certainly did not want him near them in death. Another story states that it was Moses Dustin himself who had no desire to be buried anywhere near the people of Gilmanton. In the end, no one knows the true story, but it is most likely that he was buried outside the cemetery's confines because of his color, as the practice of segregated burials was widespread in New England. Dustin was born in Canterbury in 1830 and was working as a farm laborer until the advent of the Civil War. He may have been married and had at least one child, but nothing for certain is known of his life. On August 19, 1863, he enlisted for military service in the famed all-Black Fifty-Fourth Massachusetts Regiment, the first African American regiment raised for service in the North. He served for about a year before being discharged at Penacook, New Hampshire, in August 1864 due to a problem with varicose

The gravestone of Civil War veteran Moses Dustin, Beech Grove Cemetery, Gilmanton.

veins. After the war, the remainder of his life was a transient one. He was first employed by John Kimball of Canterbury as a farmer and servant. Dustin was in Gilmanton sometime after 1880, perhaps drawn here by the prospect of work, as were others from his hometown of Canterbury. After his death in 1895, Dustin's isolated grave was marked with a military headstone, which has since the 1970s been upgraded with a modern-style military headstone. Today, Moses Dustin is no longer alone in death, with modern burials now found nearby.

The presence of the African American Cogswell family in Gilmanton began with the slaves of the Cogswell family before the American Revolution and came to an end by the 1870s. One of the last to live here was George Cogswell, who was born in 1846 and by 1860 was employed as a laborer on the farm of Lewis Prescott. Just a few years later, at the age of eighteen, he was residing in Laconia when he enlisted in the Fifty-Fourth Massachusetts Regiment on March 19, 1863, for a period of three years. Just two months later, on May 28, 1863, he was one of the regiment's one thousand men who were camped out on Boston Common in preparation for their departure to the South. Quite likely, Cogswell knew what he was getting into because, after all, Confederate authorities had made a public announcement that any captured Black soldier would be sold into slavery, while their captured white officers would be summarily executed. Private George Cogswell was subsequently among those men who took part in the famed assault on Fort Wagner at Charleston, South Carolina, on July 18, 1863 (highlighted in the 1989 movie *Glory*), by the men of the Fifty-Fourth Massachusetts, leading a vanguard of some four thousand Union troops. Sadly, Union commanders had underestimated the Confederate strength, and despite heroic fighting, the Confederates held their position. The Fifty-Fourth Massachusetts suffered heavy casualties, including the death of their leader, Colonel Robert Gould Shaw. Among the few men who were captured alive was Private Cogswell. He remained in a Confederate prison until his death on June 17, 1864, at Charleston, and today there is no memorial to his service and sacrifice.

Our final story of African American lives in this chapter concerns a family who would have a presence for over one hundred years in a town not far from the northeast shore of Lake Winnipesaukee. It began in Ossipee with a young man, Samuel Quarles, who was a graduate of the University of Michigan and returned home to be a teacher and, subsequently, a lawyer. At the age of twenty-eight, he enlisted in the Sixth New Hampshire Regiment in November 1861 for Civil War service, serving as captain of Company D. He would prove to be one of the regiment's most able officers and was severely wounded in the Battle of Spotsylvania on May 18, 1864. He was subsequently promoted to major of the regiment and then promoted for gallant and meritorious conduct to lieutenant colonel in 1865. Sometime during the course of Quarles's service, a young Black man born in Norfolk, Virginia, made his way to the Union army, likely while the regiment was somewhere near Petersburg, Virginia, between June 1864 and April 1865. The man, named Cary Wilkins, the son of Jacob and Venus Wilkins, was likely a former slave, a so-called contraband (so named because they were enemy "property" who escaped his master and made his way to the Union line. Like thousands of such men, Wilkins may have been hired as a laborer and came into contact with the men from New Hampshire while so employed. Or perhaps he first came to the Union line right where the men of the Sixth New Hampshire were stationed, but whatever the case, he would make the acquaintance of Major Quarles, who took him in and employed him as an orderly. Such roles were not uncommon for these men who came to the Union forces, but it seems clear that the former schoolteacher turned military officer took a personal interest in Wilkins's welfare. And so, when Samuel Quarles was mustered out of service in July 1865 and returned home to Ossipee, New Hampshire, he brought Cary Wilkins—said to be "black-black" in complexion—home with him. This may seem an odd choice, but it was one that was not unheard of, as a number of officers in the Union army from New England befriended and brought Black men like Wilkins, with whom they had served in close contact, home with them. Though we don't know Quarles's own thoughts on the subject, it is clear that he was a decent man and likely one who wanted to help the newly freed Wilkins in any way he could at the beginning of this new stage of his life.

So, Cary Wilkins probably came to Ossipee sometime in late 1865. At the time, he was the only Black man in Ossipee and quite possibly the only Black man in all of Carroll County. In fact, in Georgia Drew Merrill's *History of Carroll County*, written in 1889, he is the only Black person mentioned. We do not know, either, Wilkins's thoughts on his new home at first. Certainly it was an area like none he had ever seen before, and when the fall weather set in, we can imagine that Wilkins, who had lived the whole of his previous life in a much-warmer southern climate, might have had some misgivings. If so, they were likely only fleeting, as it was here, as the only Black man in town, that Cary Wilkins would stay the rest of his life. He first lived with the Quarles family and was employed as a farmhand, but on April 6, 1871, he bought an old house and farm located just up the hill from Quarles on what is now Walker Hill Road, one formerly lived in by Elder John Walker. Wilkins bought the property, located close to the county poor farm, from local resident Daniel Fall, who had owned the property for less than a year after purchasing it from Betsy Walker after the death of her husband in June 1870. Wilkins paid $100 for the property, and in return for building and maintaining the stone walls around the property (costs to be paid by Fall), Daniel Fall built a barn on the property (no longer in existence) that he maintained the right to remove "at any time." It was on this land that Wilkins would not only live the remainder of his life but where he would also start a family. In 1874, Wilkins, now age 29, married Abbie Isadore Cook (1845–1922), a white woman and native of Bartlett, New Hampshire. Together, the couple would have two children, Carrie Ernestine (1881–1980) and Erlin (1883–1976). Little now is recalled about Cary Wilkins except that he was a good farmer and a hard worker. Family records show that even in his old age, he was paid for various jobs, including "holing" (posthole digging) and working on the state roads. In April 1912, he was even paid for "picking brown tails" (what we would call cattails today, the roots of which are edible). However, his son Erlin was once a legend in town. While memories of Erlin have faded today, from his youth until his death in 1976, he was well known and respected. He would always live in the old family home on Walker Hill Road, which for years was referred to by locals as "N***** Hill," and later reminisced about his life. He attended the Brown School as a youth, but it was clear he was destined for outdoor work. He loved working in the woods and credited his mother, Abbie, for getting him started at a young age. Sometime in 1895–96, she came home with a pair of oxen she had purchased in neighboring Wolfeboro and presented them to her son, stating, "Them are yours." Erlin Wilkins would later recall that he "was tickled to death." He used those oxen for hauling a sled and to pull a mowing machine to provide hay for the family's cattle. That old iron mowing machine to this day sits on the property he hayed, over 125 years later. Erlin lived with his parents until their deaths, his father dying due to "senile disability" in 1916.

Above: The Wilkins family homestead, Walker Hill Road, Ossipee.

Left: The vintage farm machinery once pulled by the oxen owned by Erlin Wilkins of Ossipee.

Before that time, Erlin married his wife, Dora Sawyer, a native of Saco, Maine, in about 1904, and together the two would have two children, Elmer (born in 1906) and Olaf (born in 1907). Erlin was of mixed heritage and Dora was white, and while early census records list Erlin as a mulatto, later census records categorize him and his entire family as white. Though known to locals as a Black man, even if light-complexioned, he fit right in the local community and was, indeed, one of their own. Described by others late in life as a "dignified and thoughtful man," Erlin said of himself, "People will tell you, I was a rugged man." He was indeed a hard worker, getting his start at age twelve by working on old Route 16 for a "man's wage" of one dollar a day. He also worked, often with his mother in his youth, sawing, hauling, cutting, splitting and stacking wood. He worked almost any odd or handyman job you could think of, all in addition to tending to his own farm. He and his wife, Dora, made braided cotton rugs from scraps of clothing, and he would go out bee hunting. Dora was the family bookkeeper, keeping track of the wages Erlin earned and meticulously recording them. The couple also raised chickens and sold their eggs to locals and were good neighbors and citizens, helping out their older neighbors with errands, including in one case when a family was quarantined with scarlet fever and needed someone to bring them supplies. Later in life, beginning in his seventies, Erlin Wilkins would become renowned for the miles of stone walls he built all around Ossipee and Wolfeboro. He recalled that he learned this trade by watching other local masons work, and then "I got the idea how they laid their rocks and I started in on my own." This self-taught mason, to the end of his days, was renowned for his ability to look at a rock and know just how to move it at the proper fulcrum point, as well as how to fit the rocks together just so.

Later in life, Erlin Wilkins was hampered by leg and hip pain and walked with two canes. With Dora gone well before the 1970s, and with the passing of his two children, Elmer and Olaf, Erlin was left alone in the old family home, tidily kept but notable for its plastered ceiling, which was blackened by one hundred years of smoke from the old woodstove used to heat the place. In 1973, in return for being able to stay on the homestead for the remainder of his life, and with the provision that he would be provided for financially (food, utilities, medical bills, taxes, clothing, nursing home and funeral expenses) in his remaining years, Erlin Wilkins signed over the deed to the family property to Russell Bennett, a carpenter, and his wife, Gretchen. They lived just a short distance up Walker Hill Road and had been family friends for years. Cary Wilkins had even been paid some sixty years before for doing jobs for Russell's father. After the death of Erlin Wilkins on May

Left: Erlin Wilkins, circa 1950s. *Courtesy Lois Bennett Sweeney, Ossipee.*

Below: Gravestone for Cary and Abbie Wilkins, Ossipee Town Cemetery.

11, 1976, the Wilkins family name was no more. It was the end of an era. Today, the graves for Cary and Abbie Wilkins, as well as those for Erlin and Dora Wilkins, can easily be found in the Ossipee Town Cemetery, while the grave for Erlin's sister, Carrie Wilkins Eldridge, can be found not far away in the Chickville Cemetery.

Incredibly, the old Wilkins home, previously built by Elder John Walker, still exists today, found near the top of Walker Hill Road just where the pavement turns to dirt. After Erlin's death, it was owned by the Bennetts and several others for but a short time before being sold to carpenter Cal Elliot in 1980. He lovingly restored the house over the course of three years before moving in full time, and while it has modern-day conveniences on the inside, the original hewn ceiling beams are still in place, and most importantly perhaps, the outside of the home was restored to much of its period look. The original barn is long gone, a new one built in its place, but the land surrounding the old home, including the original well, looks much the same as it would have over one hundred years ago. When I drive up that way today (and it's a beautiful drive at any time of year), in my mind's eye I can spy Cary or Erlin Wilkins at the old homestead there at the top of the hill, perhaps haying the field behind a yoke of oxen or splitting a load of wood, while their wives, Abbie and Dora, are out in the yard, tending to the chickens or hanging laundry. The historian in me sees the color of their skin, but only for an instant, and what I instead envision is, quite simply, a good New Hampshire farming family through and through, who made a small but perceptible difference in their community over the course of the years.

CHAPTER 14

THE CIVIL WAR VETERANS
COME TO THE WEIRS

The numbers for New Hampshire in the Civil War are staggering: 38,943 men served in all during the war, just over 32,000 of them in regiments raised in New Hampshire alone, the rest in the marines, navy, regular army and U.S. Colored Troop regiments. Of those men who served in New Hampshire regiments, 4,840 died during the war, half of them from disease and 1,934 either killed in action or died of their wounds afterward. New Hampshire, despite its small size and population, played an oversized part in the fighting done by the Union army. Among the approximately two thousand state regimental units raised during the war for the North, three hundred of them saw the heaviest fighting and had the most casualties, including eight out of New Hampshire's twenty-one regiments. This includes the famed Fifth New Hampshire, which, according to military historian William Fox, "sustained the greatest loss in battle of any infantry or cavalry regiment, in the whole Union Army. Known to the corps and division commanders as a reliable regiment, it was more often called upon to face the enemy's fire, or assigned to the post of danger." Also included among this elite group are the Second, Third, Sixth, Seventh, Ninth, Eleventh and Twelfth New Hampshire Infantry Regiments, this last regiment being raised from towns located on or close to the shores of Lake Winnipesaukee. However, over 30,000 men *did* return home from their service, some lucky enough to have survived without a scratch, some who were wounded yet recovered in full and some, whether wounded or suffering from disease, who were broken by their service and died within months or even several years after returning home.

While the war was a cataclysmic and horrifying event in every way, for most of these men it was to be the overriding and major event in their entire life. They not only took part in an unprecedented war that was fought to save our very union, but they also, in addition to suffering hardship and witnessing up close and personal the death of friends and foe alike, were participants in a great adventure. As was true with most rank and file Civil War soldiers on both sides, their service took them far from home. Many men, especially from rural areas, probably had never even traveled fifty miles from home before, let alone one thousand miles into parts of the United States they had never before heard of or read about. And they did so in company with men for the most part from their same area, if not their own hometown. Make no mistake about it; these men were proud of what they had done, to take part in such epic battles as those at Gettysburg, Vicksburg, Antietam, Cold Harbor and on and on. They also, as all veterans do, remembered the comradery that developed in their regiment and their company and how they depended on one another in good times and bad to get the job done. In the first years after the war, harsh memories no doubt lingered, but as time passed and the horrors of battle they had experienced began to subside (the memories never go away), a feeling of nostalgia about what they had experienced gradually developed. No, such veterans would never wish to experience a war like this again, but they could look at their experiences in a different light, softened by time, and recall the good times, such as sitting by an evening campfire with their friends or the successes they had, big and small. No matter what their circumstances, these Civil War survivors constituted the largest group of veterans our country had ever seen, and within a year of the war's end, reunions among men who served in the same regiment were being organized in various parts of New Hampshire. However, it would not be until 1875 that they formally organized as the New Hampshire Veterans Association (NHVA) and held their first annual reunion and encampment in Manchester. Three years later, in 1878, they held their second reunion, this time at the Weirs in Laconia, alongside Lakeview Avenue. That encampment site, just opposite the railroad depot and next to the Weirs Beach arcade, is still owned by the NHVA today and, as it did back in 1878, has remained a place where New Hampshire's veterans can gather annually. Yet few people today, even many locals, know of its existence and historical significance.

The site, whose headquarters building is found at the junction of Lakeside and New Hampshire Avenue, was at first owned by the Boston, Concord and Montreal Railroad, which did a booming business carrying passengers to the lake as the tourist industry rapidly grew after 1850. At

Gathering of Civil War veterans at the Weirs, circa 1910, with NHVA regimental headquarters in background. *Courtesy of the New Hampshire Veterans Association.*

first the land, which was leased to the NHVA beginning in 1879 for a nominal fee, was a wooded grove next to a hotel that later became a grand establishment known as the New Hotel Weirs. Most certainly the railroad offered the land in the hope that it would gain ridership revenue from the men who traveled to this veterans' site. The railroad subsequently cleared some of the trees to build a few small roads on the site, as well as a dancing pavilion, but otherwise, veterans were housed in tents during their encampments. But not for long! After all, Civil War veterans were not getting any younger, and the prospect of sleeping outdoors in tents was probably not all that attractive. The first men to find a solution were a group of New Hampshire veterans, the Lowell Veterans Association, who were now living in Massachusetts. They built their own headquarters building, a modest Victorian-era cottage, on the encampment site in 1880, thereby providing a comfortable place for their veterans to meet and stay for the four-day encampment. The idea was a big hit, and other groups would follow suit over the next sixteen years. In all, the headquarters buildings for veterans of fourteen New Hampshire Civil War regiments would subsequently be built on the grounds (some units sharing one

The cavalry headquarters building on Lakeside Avenue, the Weirs, built in 1887.

building, others being the sole occupant) surrounding the small forest named Veterans Grove on the lot. Some of these trees are still remaining today. These buildings, which cost somewhere between $2,000 and $3,000 each to build and were constructed by local home builders, were typically paid for by shares purchased by members of the regimental associations that built them. In 1883, the famed Fifth New Hampshire built its building, followed by the Third Regiment (along with the First Band) in 1884; the Seventh Regiment in 1885; the overall regimental headquarters for the NHVA, the Second Regiment and the Manchester House (for veterans from that city) in 1886; the Sixteenth Regiment and First Cavalry buildings in 1887; the Ninth and Eleventh Regiments combined headquarters in 1888; the Eighth, Thirteenth and Fifteenth Regiments in 1889 (converting an old barracks into their combined home); and the Fourteenth Regiment in 1893. The building ended in 1896 with the addition of the combined headquarters for the men of the New Hampshire Heavy Artillery and Berdan's Sharpshooters.

In addition to these headquarter buildings, several other buildings were built on the site, including two occupied by the NHVA, one by the National

The Fifth Regiment headquarters building on Veterans Avenue, the Weirs. *Courtesy of the New Hampshire Veterans Association.*

The New Hampshire Veterans Association headquarters building, Lakeside Avenue, the Weirs. Note the fine Victorian-era trim details on the building.

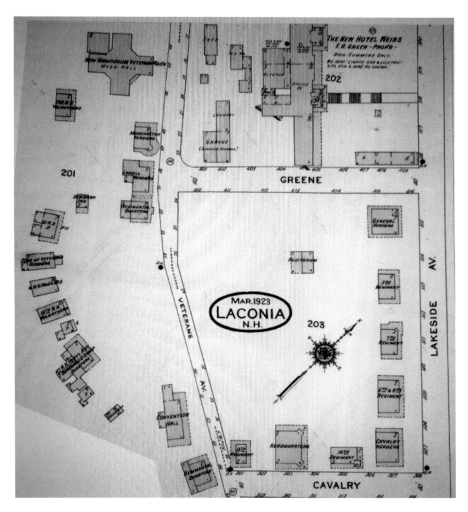

A 1923 Sanborn Company map of the NHVA site at the Weirs, which shows many buildings now lost. *Courtesy of the New Hampshire Veterans Association.*

Veteran's Association of New Hampshire and the so-called Tramp House, which was used to house veterans who came here who had no affiliation to the other regimental groups with established homes. It is said that navy veterans often stayed here, although they were also welcomed by the men who built the Ninth and Eleventh Regiment building, which explains why to this day the peak of their building facing Lakeside Avenue is adorned with a shield featuring a field of stars above an anchor and a cannon. While some of these buildings have been lost over the years due to neglect or fire, eight of them remain today. Indeed, this grouping of veteran buildings was a unique situation, and the NHVA encampment site is the only one of its kind to be permanently established for Civil War veterans in the entire country, which explains why it is in the National Register of Historic Places. The building considered to be the most complete and in near-original condition is that for the Fifteenth Regiment on Veterans Avenue toward the rear of the site, but the most famous buildings here are those that face Lakeside Avenue and Lake Winnipesaukee. In order starting from New Hampshire Avenue, these are the NHVA regimental headquarters on the corner, the Seventh Regiment building, the Ninth and Eleventh Regiment building and the First Cavalry building. Most of the buildings on this site were of the Victorian-era cottage-style type, noted for such features as their peaks, dormers, turrets, eyebrow windows and elaborate trim work, but those on the back of the property suffered more heavily over the years due to their somewhat hidden nature, and only three remain. The Fifteenth Regiment building lost its corner turret in the 1930s due to storm activity but is otherwise intact. All but one (the Third Regiment building next to the NHVA headquarters, lost by fire in 1924) of those facing Lakeview Avenue have survived and have been featured in innumerable postcards over the years, though many people today have little knowledge of their history and believe they are private residences.

As to the interior of these buildings, they were modern for their time, with indoor plumbing and kitchen facilities, but were built only for the summer months, having no insulation to make them suitable for the winter months. Indeed, they were meant to be used but once a year. Fireplaces in most were built for heating. The ground floors of the buildings had some meeting space, as well as a kitchen, bathroom and an office and bedroom that would have been reserved for use by the ranking regimental commander. The upstairs portions of these buildings were constructed dormitory style, with places where rows of cots could be placed for the rank and file members; in some cases, sheets or drapery provided the only barriers for privacy. They were not luxurious in any sense of the word, nor are they to this day, but they did provide shelter from the rain and the elements and a place to gather if the night was a cool one.

In addition to the regimental and association buildings already described, there were other buildings on the site constructed to serve the men and their activities, including a mess hall/dining facility and a pavilion or speaker's auditorium in the center, with outdoor wooden bleachers (in place until the late 1960s or so but now long gone) situated on the hillside above within the grove of trees. No doubt, for those men who perhaps preferred more creature comforts, and had the means to pay for it, the New Hotel Weirs located just across the street provided a convenient place to stay where a man and his family could visit and he could partake in all of the veteran activities before retiring in comfort at the end of the night.

The site itself is bounded by Lakeside Avenue to the north; Cavalry Avenue to the east, once running adjacent to the First Cavalry headquarters to Veterans Avenue but now no longer in existence; Veterans Avenue to the south (a dirt road now); and New Hampshire Avenue (formerly Greene Avenue), which once ran off Lakeside Avenue to the top of the hill, connecting with Veterans Avenue in front of the Lowell House. The upper part of this road past the regimental headquarters is now abandoned and closed off.

Three other features of this site also made it notable, only one of which remains. In 1883, a large forty-one-foot wrought-iron arched sign bearing the name of the NHVA was erected over New Hampshire Avenue, designed by the NHVA's longtime secretary, Major Nathaniel Shackford, who had originally enlisted as a private in the Twelfth New Hampshire Regiment before his subsequent promotion to captain and beyond beginning in 1862. When this feature was lost is not known for certain.

Another feature, this one still surviving, is the Sanborn Memorial just opposite the Lowell House at the top of New Hampshire Avenue. This site is a large boulder on which is carved the name of all of New Hampshire's Civil War regiments and enclosed by an elaborate wrought-iron fence whose pickets were fashioned in the shape of the army's Spencer Repeating Rifle, complete with affixed bayonet (these were removed some years ago, as their sharp point posed a danger to those trying to climb over the fence). The four corner posts were fashioned in the shape of a period cannon, with a cannonball on top. It is quite a stunning memorial, the whole crafted not far away at the Concord Axle Works in Fisherville, New Hampshire, one of whose founding owners was killed in action during the war. The memorial is named after Woodbury Sanborn, a native of nearby Gilford who served as a sutler (a civilian merchant) and followed the regiment during its travels and sold "food, liquor, and other comfort items" to its soldiers. Unlike many sutlers, who sometimes overcharged or swindled soldiers who had no one else to turn to for such goods while on the march, Sanborn was a man who took a personal interest in their welfare and became an honorary member of the regiment. The whole monument cost $150, the expense paid by widows, wives and daughters of the men of the Twelfth New Hampshire Regiment. It is very fitting indeed that this monument was erected in memory of someone

The unique Sanborn stone and enclosure, with pickets shaped like period rifles and corner posts in the form of cannons.

associated with that regiment; because the men of the Twelfth came from Laconia and nearby towns, their veterans had no need to build their own regimental headquarters here.

The final unusual feature was the combined statue and water trough erected at the entrance to New Hampshire Avenue. The statue portrayed Private Loammi Bean, a native of Gilford and resident of Laconia who enlisted as a private in the Eighth New Hampshire Regiment in November 1861 and was killed in action less than a year later in Louisiana on October 27, 1862, in the Battle of Georgia Landing. His daughter Nellie Bean Zebley paid for the granite-and-bronze drinking fountain and statue, and it was dedicated on August 29, 1894. On the lower level, dogs could take a drink, while a horse watering trough was located at a suitable middle level and higher up was a basin and spigot for humans, complete with drinking cups attached by chains. It stood on this site until it was struck by lightning and largely destroyed on July 23, 1931. After its shattering into numerous pieces, bystanders absconded with its various pieces to take home as either weird souvenirs or to melt down for the value of the metal. The plaque that once adorned the statue was lost for some eighty years before being rediscovered and is now in the possession of the Laconia Historical Society. There is a legend that states that the head of the statue also survived and was placed

Vintage view of New Hampshire Avenue showing the Bean statue, archway and the Lowell House at the top of the street. *Courtesy of the New Hampshire Veterans Association.*

The Fifteenth Regiment building, though now missing its corner turret, is considered the most original of the buildings at the Weirs encampment site. *Courtesy of the New Hampshire Veterans Association.*

underneath one of the regimental headquarters buildings for safekeeping, but thus far, despite diligent searches, it has yet to be found.

As to the encampments themselves, what activities and events took place? The whole event began on Tuesday and ended on Friday. On the first day, men and their families would arrive from all over by boat, train or carriage, the focal point being Weirs Landing and the railroad depot. At this location on Lakeside Avenue, period photos show thousands of people milling about on arrival, not all that different from the modern-day bike week events that are held here. The men themselves would register their arrival at the NHVA headquarters building, which was all decked out in red, white and blue bunting. At one window, the men could purchase a souvenir ribbon or program, while at another window pillows were made available to those men staying on-site for a dollar apiece. In the beginning, before the site's buildings were constructed, men stayed in tents or temporary barracks that were scattered throughout the grounds, as well as in local hotels. Once the regimental buildings were constructed, accommodations for many more men were available, though many still elected to stay in local hotels around the Weirs. Most importantly, no veteran who showed up at the encampment was ever turned away, and all were found a place to bunk, no matter where they came from. Early NHVA records show that veterans of regiments from many New England states were common attendees, though some attended from places much farther afield.

Events for each day of the encampment were planned well in advance, with a typical schedule looking something like this: reveille at 6:00 a.m. daily, followed by breakfast at 7:00 a.m. and a band concert or fife and drum corps performance from 8:00 to 10:00 a.m. Following this, each regiment held its own reunion and elected its officers for the coming year, followed by lunch at 12:30 p.m. Later, around 2:30 p.m., a grand campfire was held in the auditorium, accompanied by a band concert. Yet another campfire was held again at 7:00 p.m. It was during the campfires that the men sang the songs that they had sung years ago while off to war, popular tunes such as "Tenting on the Old Campground," "America," "Marching through Georgia" and "When Johnny Comes Marching Home," while later day favorites included "When the Boys in Blue Are Gone."

Thursday's events were often the highlight of the encampment, with a mid-morning parade organized that might include, during the peak years, nearly one thousand men. Special events were also held, especially in the early years, including mock battles being fought and artillery cannon live-firing demonstrations, while in later years a light battery of the New Hampshire National Guard fired the morning and evening guns, as well as those for special salutes. The NHVA even today has a cannon on site that is fired during special events. To get back to the schedule, later on Thursday the veterans were often visited by important personages, sometimes including the governor of New Hampshire, who gave speeches in honor of the veterans. The most important and largest of these speech-making events attended by far was that given by honorary NHVA member President Theodore Roosevelt on August 28, 1902, when he spoke to a crowd of more than twenty thousand people in Veteran's Grove. Another important historical figure who visited here was General William T. Sherman. To end each day's festivities, a military tattoo was conducted at 10:30 p.m., with Taps following at 11:00 p.m. Of course, in between all these events, and no doubt late into the night within these buildings, men could gather in smaller groups and reminisce about the "old days." As can be seen, the encampment was well organized in military style, and the grounds about were immaculately kept at all times, being "thoroughly cleansed and disinfected." The NHVA quartermaster and his assistants policed the area and kept everything and everyone in order. On Friday, the last day of events, organizational meetings were held early on, with the men afterward making ready for their departures home.

One of the focal points of each encampment was the "hero" for whom the annual event was named. This could be a soldier, from private to general, who was killed in battle or one who survived the war. Most of the encampments were named after men; the one held in 1889, for example, was named Camp E.E. Cross, in honor of Colonel Edward Cross of the Fifth New Hampshire Regiment, who was killed at the Battle of Gettysburg. However, the 1901 encampment was notable for being named in honor of Harriet Dame, a distinguished nurse who served the men from the Granite State, especially those of the Second New Hampshire Regiment, to the highest degree. The NHVA annual encampments remained a popular veterans' event for many years until participation steadily began to drop as the men of the Civil War slowly declined in numbers, with most of them gone by the 1920s. While a handful attended the encampments of the 1930s, by 1942, no Civil War veteran was present for the first time ever. In the

Public speeches and parades were among the highlights of the annual Civil War encampments at the Weirs and were attended by thousands. *Courtesy of the New Hampshire Veterans Association.*

succeeding years, encampments have continued to be held here, though the numbers have not nearly approached those in the beginning years of the NHVA. As to the later-day state of the encampment grounds, a period of decay set in as the NHVA did not have the needed funds to maintain all the headquarters buildings, but by the 1990s, after the site was placed in the National Register of Historic Places, the surviving buildings had been repaired, and preservation continues to be an ongoing focus. Indeed, their original purpose remains—to be a gathering place for veterans. New Hampshire veterans who are members of the NHVA can actually stay in these old regimental homes during the summer months with their families at a very low price despite the prime location on Lake Winnipesaukee.

Walking through these buildings today, it's not hard to imagine the veterans of over one hundred years ago who gathered here, men who experienced firsthand such historic battles as those at Cold Harbor, Chancellorsville and Gettysburg. It is at this time, perhaps, that one wishes these walls could indeed talk. So, the next time you're having fun down at the Weirs, give the old "boys in blue" a thought and stop by the NHVA headquarters. You'll connect with the Civil War in a way you never thought possible.

CHAPTER 15

THE INTERESTING BEGINNINGS OF THE *MOUNT WASHINGTON*

Our next story, at least on its surface, is not hidden at all to most of those who are acquainted with Lake Winnipesaukee. I would even go so far as to say that most folks reading this book have likely boarded the MS *Mount Washington* (MS is the designation for motorized ships) and taken a cruise around the lake, visiting its ports of call at Alton Bay, the Weirs, Wolfeboro or Meredith. However, there is much about this iconic vessel that the casual observer may not realize. While there has been much written about the *Mount Washington* that is readily available, including those books by her longtime chief purser, historian Bruce Heald of Meredith, a few facts are worth recounting here. First off, this vessel is not the original *Mount Washington* but the second vessel to bear this name on the lake. The first of them, usually referred today as the "Old Mount," was a paddle steamer launched at Alton Bay in 1872. The 187-foot-long vessel was the largest boat on the lake but was not built for the tourist trade. She was actually built as a passenger and cargo vessel, carrying up to tens of thousands of passengers every season in the days before the automobile, as well as carrying freight to and from the principal ports (listed above) on the lake and serving as a railroad connection. The working boat would continue in this role for the first fifty years of her career, but as rail transport declined and automobile and truck transportation grew exponentially by the 1920s, the SS *Mount Washington* (SS is the designation for steamships) was no longer a profitable vessel for the railroad. In the 1920s, the steamer was sold to her longtime commander, Captain Leander Lavallee. It was at this time that the

"Old Mount" was transformed into a pleasure boat, and while she would still carry a small amount of cargo, it was now the tourist trade that paid the way. This situation would remain, with the iconic steamer in service right up to the beginning of World War II. However, after the summer season of 1939 had ended, the boat was undergoing repairs at the Weirs dock, just a short distance from the Weirs Channel (and Endicott Rock), which was her normal mooring place in the wintertime. Because the lake water level was lowered at this time of the year, the steamer was grounded, and the repairs were close to being finished when a fire broke out at the Weirs railroad station on the night of December 23, 1939. Despite efforts to move the boat to safety, her grounded circumstances combined with the fast-moving fire, fueled by the wooden docks and buildings surrounding the area, doomed the *Mount Washington*, and she soon burned to the waterline, a total loss. Today, remnants of that first historic boat remain under the waters of Lake Winnipesaukee but can also be found farther away in Connecticut at the Mystic Seaport Museum.

While the loss of this iconic vessel was devastating to both Captain Lavallee and the Lakes Region as a whole, efforts were begun immediately to replace the "Old Mount" with a new one, and that's where the "hidden" part of our story begins. Today, few people viewing the boat or walking its decks, perhaps excepting old-time residents and local history enthusiasts, realize that this second *Mount Washington* was actually built, at least in part, in 1888. Captain Lavallee wanted a new boat to continue his famed service on the lake but knew that to build a new one would cost at least $250,000. Instead, the resourceful captain began to look around for another boat that could be purchased and refurbished for service on Lake Winnipesaukee. He eventually found his solution on Lake Champlain in Vermont, for it was here that he found the iron hull of the old paddlewheel steamer *Chateaugay*. This vessel was built at Shelburne, Vermont, in 1888, her iron hull fashioned by the well-known firm of Harlan & Hollingsworth in Wilmington, Delaware. The boat was 195 feet long on the keel and 203 feet long overall, coming in at 724 gross tons. Built as a passenger vessel for the Champlain Transportation Company, *Chateaugay*'s career on Lake Champlain lasted for years. She was noted "as an excellent boat, elegantly fitted up and of fine speed." In many ways, her early career was very similar to that of the *Mount Washington*. By 1939, however, she, too, was in the twilight of her career. Deemed obsolete just like the "Old Mount" in the 1920s, she was moored at the Burlington Yacht Club, serving as their clubhouse. Captain Lavallee subsequently negotiated the purchase of the hull of the old *Chateaugay* for $20,000 and had

Top: The 1888 hull of the former Vermont steamer *Chateaugay* served as the basis for today's *Mount Washington*. *Courtesy Library of Congress*.

Bottom: Today's *Mount Washington* plies the waters of Lake Winnipesaukee between the major ports just as her original namesake did.

it cut into twenty sections and shipped back to Lakeport, New Hampshire, by rail to serve as the basis of the *Mount Washington II* (as this successor ship was first named).

Here, John Alden and the men of the General Ship and Engine Works of East Boston built a new *Mount Washington* on the old 1888 hull of the *Chateaugay*. Since Captain Lavallee desired a steam engine, which type of power plant was no longer being built, further searches had to be made for them. They finally found it in the hull of an old steam yacht, the *Crescent III*, in New York. Purchased for $25,000, this vessel's steam engines were used in the new *Mount Washington*. The work proceeded very quickly, with an extraordinary amount of local interest and help, and in August 1940, she was launched into the waters of Lake Winnipesaukee, less than a year after that disastrous fire. Since that time, except for the wartime years of 1942–45, when her engines were requisitioned for use in a U.S. Navy ship, the *Mount Washington* has sailed the waters of the big lake every summer.

No, the *Mount Washington* of today is not exactly the same boat as that which was built in 1940 in less than eight months' time; new diesel engines were installed after the war in the spring of 1946, all her steam equipment is now gone and these engines, now worn out, were subsequently replaced with new Caterpillar diesel engines in 2010. Also, in 1982 the hull of the *Mount Washington* was cut open and increased in size by twenty feet to improve her passenger accommodations. However, despite all these changes, the iron hull of the *Chateaugay* remains as strong and solid as ever. The *Mount Washington*, through the long years from 1946 to today, has remained a popular tourist attraction on the lake, a true icon, all of this made possible by an iron hull fashioned in 1888.

CHAPTER 16

THE END OF AN ERA IN EDUCATION

I f you love historic architecture in a beautiful rural setting, Gilmanton is the town for you. Once one of the most prominent towns in the state, it has a number of very fine colonial-era homes, a historic tavern, four historic churches, a historic schoolhouse and the old town hall in Gilmanton Ironworks that are all well worthy of a visit. However, perhaps the most prominent structure in town is a building that is very well known to locals and one that is part of Gilmanton's everyday work life, the Gilmanton Town Hall, located at 503 Province Road in the Gilmanton Four Corners part of town. It is quite a grand and impressive structure that is temple-like in appearance, more so than most town halls in rural New Hampshire, but there's a reason for that, one that is hidden to the casual observer. For you see, this building, which has served as the town hall since 1989, wasn't built at all for that purpose but instead was once the home of the prestigious Gilmanton Academy school, and at its completion in 1895, it was one of the last of its kind to be built in New Hampshire.

The beginnings of the Gilmanton Academy came in 1792 when a group of prominent men in town, those who "looked beyond common school instruction," came up with the idea of establishing a "higher branch of education" in Gilmanton. At this time in New Hampshire and elsewhere in New England, primary education was the sole focus of public schooling. The basics of reading, writing and arithmetic were offered in small, one-room schoolhouses like that at Kelly Corner in Gilmanton. This basic education was suitable for many young men who might pursue a living as a farmer or blacksmith, but for those few students, usually the sons of the wealthiest in town, who wished to pursue a professional career as a minister, lawyer, teacher or doctor, a secondary education was required. This usually came in the form of private tutoring from a man who was already a practitioner in one of these professions, perhaps one in town if they were lucky, but in many rural areas, this usually meant journeying to a larger city. Once this tutoring was complete, the young man in question would then be ready for college at an institution like Dartmouth or Harvard. However, with the establishment of the academy system of secondary education in the late eighteenth century, local institutions of higher learning (what we might call a college prep school today) became popular and were established in many New Hampshire towns. These were not just in the larger and more prominent towns like Portsmouth and Exeter on the seacoast but also in a number of rural towns.

It is not surprising that Gilmanton established its own academy, as the town, despite its rural character today, was one of the largest and most important towns in the state outside the seacoast area by the time of the American Revolution. The town committee established in 1792 to explore the idea of establishing an academy was authorized to open a subscription, the idea that "an Academy in town would be useful to the inhabitants" winning the day. Two years later, in June 1794, the state legislature granted a charter for Gilmanton Academy. The "design of the institution of said Academy, is to encourage and promote virtue, and piety, and the knowledge of the English, Greek, and Latin languages, Mathematics, Writing, Geography, Logic, Oratory, Rhetoric, and other useful and ornamental branches of Literature." The academy was to be run by a board of trustees and overseers, and the property held by the academy would be free of taxes as long as its value did not exceed $3,300, a hefty sum at the time. The charter also stipulated that no student would be free of taxes or military duty until enrolled in the academy for at least nine months.

With the legal details worked out over the next few years, the first Gilmanton Academy school structure was built on land once owned by Joseph Badger Jr. (one of the founding trustees) beginning in 1797, and the first classes were held in December 1797. The first "preceptor" or headmaster was a local man, Peter Folsom, who was a Dartmouth graduate. Early tuition rates were set at about $1.50 per quarter, subsequently raised to $2.00 in 1806 and $3.00 in 1814. At first, only male students were accepted, but this changed in 1814, when the Gilmanton Academy hired its first female preceptor, Ann W. Clarke, a native of Hancock, New Hampshire, and a graduate of the Bradford Academy.

In January 1808, the first Gilmanton Academy building burned down, but it was replaced with a new structure within several months. The town offered money to help with rebuilding costs, in return being allowed to hold town meetings in the upper story of the building. The academy was also helped the following year when, in June 1809, the so-called Atkinson and Gilmanton Academy Grant of land, comprising some nineteen thousand acres in the far northeast part of New Hampshire, was made to these two academies on an equal basis by the State of New Hampshire. In this unusual arrangement with the state, it was hoped that the area would eventually be settled and economic development furthered. The academies, in theory, would reap the benefits from the sale of parcels of land within the grant. The Dartmouth College Grant was also made with a similar goal, but for the Atkinson and Gilmanton Academies, this land was never settled to a great degree, and even today, at least as of the 2010 census, not one single person is recorded as living in the area of the grant.

Among the other interesting details about Gilmanton Academy in its early years of operations that have been recorded by town historian Reverend Daniel Lancaster, himself an official at the academy like other town ministers through the years, include the fact that in 1828, pews in the Congregational church (located next door) and in the town's Methodist church were purchased by the academy for "the use of scholars," while in 1829, four "pious" and "indigent" students had their tuition "remitted," a nice indicator that the trustees of the academy did not just take into account financial standing when admitting students. In 1835, Gilmanton Academy expanded its schooling by establishing a theology department due to the fact that many of its students went on to become clergymen. In 1836, a seminary was established, with a separate large Seminary Hall built nearby to accommodate their students, which was dedicated in 1841. The seminary of Gilmanton Academy was short-lived, however, and was out of business by 1846.

The Gilmanton Academy remained a prominent educational institute both in town and the surrounding area for years, amassing a one-thousand-volume library, as well as a significant collection of scientific equipment and even a cabinet containing five hundred mineral specimens. The academy was also a large part of the social fabric of the town for its entire existence. Various exhibitions were put on by the school itself, while entertainment events like plays and even an opera were put on by the students themselves, with the proceeds for the sale of tickets to these events providing a source of income for the groups involved. And when the facilities of the academy were not being used for official purposes, the hall in the academy was sometimes rented out to traveling theater companies and for town events. Indeed, as one minister commented, Gilmanton Academy was both a "font of science" and a "muse of thought."

As to alumni, the Gilmanton Academy counted many future ministers and teachers among its graduates but also two interesting local men, one who represented the best of Gilmanton society and one who would leave New Hampshire to eventually make a name for himself, but not in a good way. William Badger served two terms (each lasting a year) as the fifteenth governor of New Hampshire from 1834 to 1836 and was a trustee and president of the academy. But Herman Mudgett, graduate of the class of 1881, would later go on to medical school before becoming a serial killer, going under the now famous alias of H.H. Holmes during his killing spree in Chicago during the 1893 World's Fair and beyond.

The Gilmanton Academy continued in operation for many years, but disaster struck again when the building and most of its assets were destroyed by a large fire that occurred on May 24, 1894, when the academy was

The 1895-built Gilmanton Academy building now serves as the Gilmanton Town Hall, its school days long past.

celebrating the centennial of its founding. Nearly everything the academy owned, all its furnishings and most of its large library included, was lost. Among the saved items were three hundred recently donated library volumes, pulled from the fire by Principal S.W. Robertson. However, almost immediately, plans to build a new academy building commenced, and within eight months, on January 18, 1895, the current Gilmanton Academy building that now serves as the town hall was complete and ready to use. The speed with which the new academy building was made a reality is a true testament to the area's devotion to higher education. The new building cost just $5,800, a bargain made possible by the fact that the architectural firm of Bodwell & Sargent in Concord drew up the plans free of charge, while builder Gardner Cook of Laconia did the job at a below-market price because he was a graduate of the academy.

However, while a new building was now in place to serve Gilmanton Academy, the times were changing and would soon leave the institution in its wake. With the rise of the public high school system in New Hampshire by the end of the nineteenth century, combined with the rise of more prestigious boarding schools, institutions like the Gilmanton Academy could not survive, and the academy system faded away. Indeed, architectural historian David Ruell has speculated that the surviving Gilmanton Academy building was probably one of the last, if not the last, of the academy buildings built in New Hampshire. The Gilmanton Academy lasted only another fifteen years, graduating its final class in 1910. Efforts were made to revive the school over the next few years, but these came to naught. The final blow came in 1916 when the Town of Gilmanton established its own high school. But all was not lost, as the building was first used by the new high school beginning in 1916 and later used to house an elementary school before going out of educational service for good in 1966. It is interesting to note that the trustees of Gilmanton Academy retained ownership of the school for many years, leasing it to the town, but finally, in 1948, gave the property and its remaining funds to the town's school department.

From 1967 to 1987, the old academy building was used sporadically for some functions and did house a small historical museum, but when it became clear that Gilmanton needed a new home for its town offices, as the Old Town Hall at the Ironworks was badly in need of refurbishing, the town decided, after much study, to use the old Gilmanton Academy building as its new home. In 1989, with some interior modifications, the new town hall opened in the Gilmanton Academy building, and here it has remained to this day. The wood-framed building itself is a notable example of a Colonial

Revival–style structure, highlighted by its hip-roofed main building flanked by side and rear wings that highlight the five different rooflines of the building and an octagonal cupola. However, it is the façade of the building that really stands out, highlighted by the steep pediment above and towering corner and central pilasters topped with ornate capitals and, of course, the large round central window that looks like a globe. Temple-like in appearance, the Gilmanton Town Hall today really does stand out as a monument to the importance and high esteem in which higher education was held in this part of the Lakes Region for well over one hundred years.

CHAPTER 17

REMINDERS OF THE IRON HORSE

O nce upon a time, until about ninety years ago, it was not the automobile that brought visitors to many of the towns around Lake Winnipesaukee but the railroad. It's hard to picture such towns as Alton, Meredith or Wolfeboro in the olden and, perhaps, more quiet days, but prior to the coming of the "iron horse," travel was by carriage or stagecoach, and while tourists were starting to make their way here by the 1830s, it would be the coming of the railroad that made the tourist trade what it is today. It all started with the Boston, Concord and Montreal Railroad, which was formed in 1844 and began construction of its main line at Concord in 1846. Two years later, in 1848, the railroad arrived in Laconia, spurring great economic growth and tourism in the process. From this time forward, the railroads played a great part in transforming the region into a summertime playground for folks from all over New Hampshire, New England, New York and beyond. Remnants of the railroad can easily be seen, and even experienced, in several different ways. First and foremost, you can ride a portion of the old rails of the Boston, Concord and Montreal on the Winnipesaukee Scenic Railroad, a tourist train that runs on some twelve miles of track in the summer and fall season between Meredith and the Weirs. The trip lasts an hour or two and is well worth the experience in its vintage passenger cars, some of which date back to the 1920s. The primary architectural evidence of the railroads and their former glory are the many old train depots that can be found in such towns as Wolfeboro, Alton, Laconia and the Weirs. Some of these remaining historic structures still serve the public today, while other, smaller depots are privately owned, and some have even been turned into residences. Yet another reminder of the railroads are the rail-trails or recreational paths that follow old railroad tracks that can be found in the Lakes Region, including the WOW (Winnipesaukee, Opechee, Winnisquam) Trail that runs from Lakeport to the Belmont town line and the Cotton Valley Rail-Trail, which runs twelve miles from downtown Wolfeboro to Wakefield on the route of the old Wolfeborough Railroad. Of all these different remnants of the railroads, two of them—one in plain view and one just off the beaten path—have a hidden history all their own that is quite fascinating and worthy of a closer look.

The oldest of these sites is found on the Letter S Road in Alton, a very short distance from downtown Alton as the crow flies, and not far from the headwaters of Alton Bay. If you travel on Main Street (Route 11) heading out of town toward Alton Bay and turn left on Letter S Road, you will soon come to a major bend in the road, and it is at that bend that you will see, on either side of the road, two towering masonry structures. Stop here, just before or beyond, by the side of the Merrymeeting River, and if you look across the river, you'll see another similar stone structure on the embankment. It was here that the tracks of the Dover and Winnipisseogee Railroad (yes, its name incorporated one of the innumerable versions of the name "Winnipesaukee") crossed the Merrymeeting River on its way to Alton Bay just a short distance beyond. The river today may not look so imposing, but it was nonetheless a major crossing for the railroad, the longest bridge on the entire line, measuring 130 feet long overall, its main span measuring about 94 feet. The railroad, originally known as the Cocheco Railroad, had its beginnings in 1839 when it received its first charter, but efforts to get the business underway failed. It was chartered again in 1847 and this time got off the ground, its tracks reaching neighboring Farmington in 1849. By 1851, it had finally reached Alton Bay. The tracks were supposed to be continued to Meredith, but this goal was never reached, and Alton Bay became its terminus. The bridge over the Merrymeeting River was built in 1851, but little is known about its construction. It was likely originally a wooden structure, as iron was not yet in common use for New England railroad bridges, it being both more expensive and truss designs still evolving. However, the original bridge was rebuilt in 1887 of iron construction (steel was not yet so commonly used) and was of the double-Warren deck truss type, with the tracks running on top of the bridge. The Warren truss design, noted for the triangular configuration of its members, was patented in 1848 and by the 1880s was a tried and true bridge form, a true investment in the local infrastructure. With this bridge in place, the line's twenty-ton locomotive *Alton Bay* (built by the Taunton Locomotive Works at a cost of $6,850) could chug the remainder of the distance to Alton Bay. From there, the excursion steamer *Dover* would carry passengers and some freight to Wolfeboro and back, but the service was never very profitable, as the freight business from Lake Winnipesaukee back to Dover never materialized to any great degree. This was due in large part to the fact that the railroad was denied access and connection at the Weirs and the commercial opportunities in Laconia because that port was the territory of the rival Boston, Concord and Montreal Railroad. With increasing financial pressures, the Dover and Winnipisseogee Railroad was leased to the Boston and Maine Railroad in 1872, and by 1892, it was entirely absorbed by that giant. Freight traffic was long gone, and passenger rail service to Alton, consisting primarily of camp meeting visitors and summer tourists, slowed greatly by the 1920s as a result of the growth of automobile travel and finally ceased by 1935. As to the exact date when the bridge over the Merrymeeting River was finally dismantled, this is unknown but likely occurred within a few short years. However, still left in place all these long years since are the supports of the bridge. In 2016, the so-called Letter S Road Railroad Trestle Supports were added to the New Hampshire State Register of Historic Places through the efforts of local historian Marty Cornelissen of the Alton Historical Society. So, the next time you get a chance, take a drive down the Letter S Road in Alton. I'll bet you can imagine that old locomotive thundering across the Merrymeeting River, carrying a carload or two of passengers ready to start their summer vacation.

Our second railroad feature of note is hardly hidden at all, yet one part of its history is all but unknown except to local historians and railroad buffs. In the heart of downtown Wolfeboro is one of the town's most recognizable features, the 1872-built Wolfeborough Station railroad depot located at the head of Railroad Avenue in Depot Square. Most people today believe that this station was the end of the line of the Wolfeborough Railroad. This railroad line, which ran twelve short miles from Wolfeboro Junction (now Sanbornville), was formally established in 1868 and constructed in 1871–72. It was leased by the Eastern Railroad in 1872 and later taken over by the Boston and Maine Railroad in 1884. However, the Wolfeborough Station was not the end of line; the tracks actually continued across Main Street and ended at the town docks. Yes, you read correctly—the trains crossed (and sometimes blocked!) Main Street and ran right down to the waterfront, where both passengers and freight were offloaded for embarkation on boats like the

Postcard view, circa 1910, of the Merrymeeting River railroad bridge in Alton. The Letter S Road and remaining abutments are visible at center left.

The historic Letter S Road trestles are all that remain of the old Dover and Winnipisseogee Railroad, which made it to Alton Bay in 1851.

Mount Washington steamer to make the passage to other Lake Winnipesaukee ports. Indeed, if you think crowds and heavy traffic are a problem in Wolfeboro today, where the summer population expands from just over six thousand people to upward of twenty thousand people at any given time in the height of summer, they were pretty large even 150 years ago. Those passengers waiting for a lake steamer originally gathered in the waiting room of the old Boston and Maine wharf-side building, but after that building was destroyed by a disastrous fire in May 1899, a new solution was needed. In 1900, the problem was solved when the Lake Station was built. Visitors and locals alike know this building today as the Dockside Restaurant. As period postcards show, locomotives would arrive here head-on, facing the lake, and after unloading passengers and freight, the train would then back up the short distance to the area of the Wolfeborough Station, where it would then turn around as it departed town for Wolfeborough Junction. It is pretty interesting today to think of all this heavy railroad equipment maneuvering around in the confined space of downtown Wolfeboro, but it was a situation that would prevail for some thirty-five years or so. However, by the 1930s, as automobile travel inexorably overtook train travel, ridership and freight traffic went into a severe decline, and in 1935, the Lake Station was closed

A postcard view, circa 1910, of a Wolfeboro Railroad locomotive at the Lake Station depot, with passengers waiting for the *Mount Washington*.

for good. The Boston and Maine Railroad would discontinue passenger trains on the Wolfeboro (as the town name by this time was spelled) line in 1936 but would continue running mixed passenger and freight trains until 1950, with a limited amount of freight service continuing on the line into the 1960s. Once this service ended, the line, as many locals can still remember, was revived as a heritage/tourist railroad, which was in operation from 1973 to 1978 and again from 1980 to 1985 until train service finally ceased for all time. While the trains have been gone for many years now, the Lake Station remains and, in fact, has had a life as a local restaurant since 1948, serving up good food for over seventy years now—more than double the time it served the railroad. Sitting at the Dockside Restaurant today in the summertime, you can still see the *Mount Washington* come and go from Wolfeboro Bay at regular intervals, just like the visitors of old once did. Some things never change, though the locomotives that once idled right by the town docks are now but a distant memory.

Chapter 18
Good Intentions Gone Awry in Laconia

There are some aspects of our history, those that are unusual, interesting or significant milestones, that everyone wants to celebrate. This is the history we are glad or proud to share collectively. And then there are those aspects of our history, equally interesting and significant, that highlight events that are controversial, sad, disturbing or even embarrassing. This is the darker side of history if you will, the events that make us question who we are, or were, as a people and give us pause to wonder how such things ever came to be. Every community, every state, every country has had such events in its historical past, be they big or small, left hidden in the mists of time or brought out into the open and debated. It's an inescapable aspect of the past, for in human history we must always look to both the good and the bad if we are to understand how we got to where we're at today. For the Lakes Region, and for New Hampshire as a whole, one of the darker aspects of our history is the Laconia State School. While this chapter in New Hampshire history ultimately may be seen as having a good ending, to this day many historians and healthcare professionals alike can't help but wonder how and why it took so long to get there. In all honesty, this is not a "feel-good" story, nor is it for the faint of heart. However, it is a necessary one, if only to serve as a reminder of the past in the hopes that we don't make similar mistakes in the future.

In February 1901, the New Hampshire Federation of Women's Clubs wrote to the New Hampshire state legislature, calling for action on what to them was an item of vital interest. In speaking about those individuals

One of a number of abandoned dormitory buildings on the site of the Laconia State School.

in society who were developmentally disabled (then called "feebleminded), they wrote, "As a simple act of justice, is it right for the state to cast off those, who through no fault of theirs, are lacking in mental equipment?" They sought to have a special school established where such "feebleminded" individuals, primarily children, could be placed. However, later in their plea, they get to the real heart of the matter, further stating, "As an act of self-protection, is it not the part of wisdom to guard society from the crimes, the vice, and the immorality of this degenerate class, who with their weak will-power and deficient judgement are easily influenced by evil?" So much for having the best interests of this vulnerable class of individuals as the main concern. Now, to be fair to the women of New Hampshire, they were just echoing the rising idea in the community at large of establishing an institution to house the feeble-minded that was also popular in the medical community and was reflective of what had already been done in Massachusetts, our neighbor to the south. And so it was that later in 1901, legislation was passed authorizing the formation of the New Hampshire School for the Feeble-Minded. Eventually, some 247 acres of farmland, on which sat several buildings, including a house and barn, were purchased from the Crockett family in Laconia to serve as the site of this specialized school, located on North Main Street (Route 106) in a beautiful spot overlooking the end of Opechee Bay, accessed today by turning onto the ironically named Right Way Path Road. It is quite interesting that before the school was built here, a number of towns vied for the honor of having the school built in their community, but Laconia was the so-called winner. The school was opened in 1903 with sixty children admitted from area almshouses and poor farms, and by 1910, there were a number of buildings on its grounds and surrounding farmland. These included, in addition to the farm buildings, a hospital, a dormitory, a combined dormitory and dining hall and service buildings like a laundry and boiler house. A number of these buildings are in existence to this day, and even though access to the currently abandoned site is limited, one can get an idea of the layout and size of the place by walking on foot. The first "inmates," as the disabled in the school were referred to, were children between the ages of three and twenty-one, and in the early years, the average age at the time of admission was eleven years old. Sadly, by their very designation as "inmates," we can see that the only "crime" these innocent children had committed was to be different from the rest of society for reasons outside their own control.

One major question that arises is this: where were the developmentally disabled cared for in the days before the school was established? Well, many had been cared for at home, but others were also housed at places like almshouses for the poor or county poor farms. Indeed, prior to the establishment of the school in Laconia, it had been traditionally the job of each individual town or county to care for those in society who could not care for themselves. This included not just the disabled but also the indigent and poor, unwed mothers with children, those chronically out of work for any number of reasons—in short, those on the lowest rung of society's ladder. However, such town and county almshouses were often haphazardly run, and people could come and go at will. People's attitudes, too, were changing as Darwin's theories on evolution became more widely known, and it was in the late 1800s that ideas about the nature of heredity began to affect how the poor were viewed by scientists and doctors. Put simply, the poor and disabled were said to be so because it was part of their genetic makeup, and thus they began to be seen less as human beings and more as a drag on society as a whole. The idea of institutionalizing and better controlling this "diseased" class of the population was seen as the best solution for society. Within a short time, these ideas would evolve even further and take a more sinister turn toward eugenics.

Few people realize that eugenics were practiced in New Hampshire (and elsewhere in the United States); the school began a sterilization program (with two-thirds involved being women) in 1917. This program was conducted under the guidance of school head Dr. Benjamin Baker, who was a full-on believer in eugenics. At first, such sterilizations were done with the consent of the patient or their family, but by 1929, the law had been changed to allow the school unlimited powers in this regard. Many—likely most—such procedures were performed on an involuntary or, at best, a coerced basis. In fact, for those residents who wished to leave the school, sterilization was mandatory in order for a release to be made. By 1947, 264 sterilizations had been performed, and over 400 such procedures occurred before they ceased in 1958, and only then because of the increasingly publicized accounts of the horrifying eugenics experiments practiced by the Nazis during World War II at such notorious places as Auschwitz. When the New Hampshire press began to make those comparisons regarding the Laconia State School, that kind of publicity resulted in change. While some residents of the school did leave under varying circumstances, not all did, and an unknown number, likely over two hundred, died here over the years. Residents of the school who died were first buried on the grounds of the school in unmarked graves, but this changed when the Laconia State School Cemetery was established on Chemung Road in Meredith. All burials here were at first unmarked until 1978, when parents of the residents organized and facilitated the purchase of small metal plaques on granite markers, with names and years of birth and death, to mark each grave. As to the unmarked graves around the school, no one knows where they are located, though one former foreman on the farm told historian and former Laconia State School official Gordon Dubois during his research that when he first started work on the school farm, he was told not to plow the farm fields too deep: "You never know what you're going to find buried there."

By 1906, there were 82 "inmates" at the New Hampshire School for the Feeble-Minded, and ten years later, that number had increased to 293. At first only children were admitted, but later women over the age of twenty-one were accepted, and eventually people of all ages were allowed. Almost always through the years, waiting lists for new "inmates" was long. How did these admittances to the school come about? In many cases, they were done on a doctor's recommendation. Families with disabled children were advised in some cases to admit them and forget about them altogether, as if they had never existed. In other cases, those who were once cared for at home were admitted here because the family no longer had the resources to care for them, parents had become too aged to take care of their disabled children any longer or a sudden death had left such individuals with no one else to care for them. In almost no case, if any, were admittances to the school deemed a happy occasion, and some former residents or parents even to this day can recall the cries and screams of anguish that could be heard as a parent departed the grounds of the school after having committed their loved one.

In the beginning, there was little supervision of the residents at the school, whose name was changed to the Laconia State School in 1924. The years between the two world wars were most difficult, especially during the years of the Great Depression, when some families were anxious to get rid of extra mouths to feed and the school itself did not have enough resources to adequately provide for everyone. As to programs at the "school," activist Freda Smith (whose own daughter was a resident for a time) would later state that "the very name was deceptive. There was no schooling, there was no training. People just existed in that sterile environment. In reality, it was a warehouse for human beings." In fact, by 1914, the population of the school had grown to 614 people. As to what did go in inside the school, there were several classes of individuals. Those who were capable of working did so on the institution's farm or in other support buildings like the cafeteria or laundry facilities.

Food-wise, it was hoped that the "inmates" working the institution's farm and caring for its dairy herd would make it self-sufficient, and in effect, inmates worked for their food and room and board, receiving no real pay for their work. These practices endured until the farm closed in 1968 and the cows were sold off in 1970, but the slowly deteriorating barns can still be seen today from the main road. Those who were severely disabled and unable to work were cared for by two groups, including the female inmates of age to do so, as well as a staff that was stretched so thin that each person was responsible for thirty to fifty people at any given time. Often residents wandered the halls of the large buildings at random and were unsupervised or, after 1952 when a television set was donated, sat in front of the TV all day. The staff at the Laconia State School was indeed challenged, not having enough training or the needed resources to do their job. Many were kind and loved their patients, but it must be noted that, by accounts from former residents, others on the staff were cruel to the patients. Many residents were verbally abused and talked about derogatorily in front of their faces. Others

Abandoned farmhouse and greenhouse on the site of the Laconia State School.

were physically abused, being slapped or hit in the face, hair pulled and even pushed down flights of stairs. Even more disturbing, some residents were sexually assaulted. Sadly, even medical doctors, when performing simple procedures, refused to administer sedatives to ease the pain, stating that "they're not like us." One resident even recalled that they were given undignified and bizarre haircuts, with one half of the head shaved and the other left as is, so that they could be identified in public if they ever ran away. Former resident Samantha Chamberlain stated succinctly during her interview for the film *Lost in Laconia*, "Your dignity and rights were pulled away from you."

It is not surprising that later on, when efforts to change the school were underway, it was deemed a place worse than the state prison, "a huge blemish" on New Hampshire's reputation. Indeed, the state was culpable for these conditions, and not just due to a lack of oversight but also the ever-present problem of allocating too few resources. One legislator even stated, when the restroom facilities were in dire need of repair, that such expenses were "a waste of money," as the residents would not know how to operate the new toilets. Sadly, even the basic necessities of food and clothing were

The old dairy barns at the Laconia State School, where residents were employed to make the school self-sufficient.

lacking at the school for many years. Residents often did not have enough food, and what was served was often done so from unsanitary and outdated facilities. By the time it reached residents, it was often cold to the touch. Clothing was also a huge problem for the school for most of its existence. Residents usually only wore their own clothing one time; afterward, it went into the general laundry facilities and then returned willy-nilly to the general population. Residents wore what was available, even if clothing was ill-sized or unmatched. Due to a lack of staffing, many residents simply wandered around naked. Many residents went barefoot, even in the winter on the cold tile floors, as the cloth slippers that were provided were often in short supply. As to living conditions, residents were usually housed dormitory style in large rooms with eighty or so beds. The rooms were cold and drafty, and the windows usually had no curtains. With very few exceptions, there was no privacy, no personal possessions and no comfortable places to sit or relax. Benches were used because they could easily be hosed down. Toilet and shower facilities were also substandard, with large groups of the same sex showering and going to the bathroom together. There were no shower curtains or toilet stalls.

The conditions at the Laconia State School remained "grim" but would begin to change when new superintendent Richard Hungerford arrived in 1953. He was the first school leader to be an educator, rather than a doctor, and right away he saw the need for reform. During his seven-year tenure, he was a trailblazer, best known for inviting parents to the school and empowering them as "reform agents," advising them that only by their activism could things at the school be changed for the good. Indeed, it has been said that Hungerford was the first in the nation to recognize the political power of parents, and he put them to good use, inviting them to film conditions in the school. This movie was made public in 1956. It was also during his tenure that the New Hampshire Coalition for Retarded Children was established in 1953, as well as the New Hampshire Association for Retarded Citizens. By 1955, such groups were holding national fundraisers to raise awareness about the developmentally disabled and their civil rights, or lack thereof. Hungerford actually lobbied the state to amend its laws to include residents of the school to be designated as "handicapped" and fought for mandatory educational guidelines, as well as for resources for the school. In fact, Hungerford and his pioneering efforts would make him an enemy to the New Hampshire state government, but by the time of his forced resignation in 1960, he not only raised awareness but also enacted coed activities at

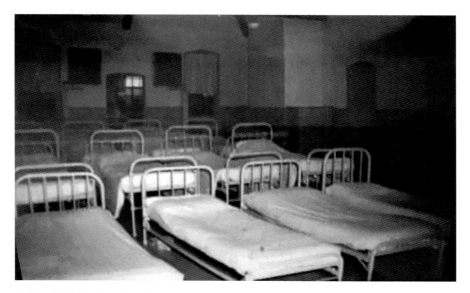

A circa 1960 interior view of the cramped and non-private dormitory-style sleeping arrangements for residents at the Laconia State School.

the school, built a geriatrics building and established summer workshops for teachers at the school that helped them learn how to teach disabled children. Such measures seem so simple in our day and age, but back in the 1950s, this was progressive stuff that Hungerford was advocating, and it was improving the lot of the residents of the Laconia State School bit by bit.

After Hungerford's departure, the school would backslide a bit, the focus once more on the medical side of things, with many residents heavily medicated. By the era of President John F. Kennedy in 1962, there were 990 residents at the school, but with the president's signing of the landmark Community Mental Health Act in October 1963 and the focus on community rather than institutionalized care, things would gradually change in Laconia. Living conditions at the now-aged school were "desolate" by the 1970s, when there were 1,000 residents, but community programs had been established and even a foster grandparent program. In 1975, a law was passed that gave rights to the residents for "adequate and humane" living conditions and treatment, and in 1978, the landmark *Garrity v. Gallen* (Hugh Gallen, the governor of New Hampshire) case resulted in court orders to reduce the population at the Laconia State School. It also led to the establishment of the area agency system in New Hampshire of caring for the developmentally disabled in a community setting. Within twelve years, there were fewer than 100 residents at the Laconia State School, and on January 31, 1991, the state school closed for good, ending its ninety-eight-year history. New Hampshire has the distinction, despite the troubled history of the Laconia State School, of being the first state in the nation to eliminate institutionalized care.

While the Laconia State School closed in 1991, the buildings of the institution would remain in use and its checkered history would continue. Later in 1991, the site was converted to the Lakes Region Facility, a state prison, with the number of inmates (true inmates this time) limited to three hundred and only those who had committed certain, lesser crimes transferred here. Indeed, due to community displeasure, few in Laconia wanted the facility (a far cry from when the facility was first built), but with pressures on the state prison, the number of inmates rose to five hundred in 1997 and eventually to six hundred. It was inmate labor that was largely used to help renovate the buildings of the old school for use as a prison, which accounts for its foreboding barbed-wire appearance today. In 2004, the facility became a transitional one for inmates soon to be paroled, and finally, in 2009, the prison was closed for good. Its antiquated and poor conditions ranked it as the least efficient prison in the state at the time. Since that time, it has remained dormant, its buildings slowly continuing to deteriorate. There is much debate about what to do with the large site, with the state expending millions of dollars over the last twelve years to maintain and secure it. Historic surveys of the buildings on the site have been conducted. Family members of former residents of the Laconia State School and other organizations have heavily advocated for the placement of a memorial of some kind, while others propose that one of the buildings on the site could be converted to a museum of sorts to house an archive of documents related to the Laconia State School. Both are excellent ideas that should be acted upon, but in the meantime, the abandoned site sits in limbo, waiting for something to happen, not unlike the condition it left its thousands of "inmates" in for many long and lonely years.

CHAPTER 19

A TALE OF THREE TOWERS

The Lakes Region is one of the most beautiful in the entire state, and at a number of places around Lake Winnipesaukee, there are excellent opportunities to get a good aerial view of the scenery. One of the most unique ways to access these stunning vistas is by climbing the several historic fire or observation towers that are located around the lake in Gilford, Moultonborough and Tuftonboro. All of them have a history of ninety years or more of service, and each of them is easy to find and requires but an easy to moderate hike to access. The oldest of these towers is the fire observation tower found atop 2,378-foot-high Belknap Mountain in Gilford. It was first built in 1913 and was part of a network of fire towers built around the state beginning in 1903. It can be accessed by taking Belknap Mountain Road off Route 11A and subsequently turning on Carriage Road, a dirt road that leads to a large parking area where trails to the summit begin. While such towers in the United States were first built in the West, New Hampshire was the first state in the East to build them. These structures were important in the fight against forest fires. The state Forestry Commission began building its own structures in increasing numbers as funds became available in 1909 and eventually acquired others that were built by the New Hampshire Timberland Owners Association. Of course, the prevention of forest fires was an important part in maintaining the state's forestry business.

Many of these towers were first built of wood and had simple ladders to get to the top, the upper enclosed part of the towers, known as the "cab," which was equipped with telephones so that any fires spotted could be quickly reported. Later on, however, the towers across the state were rebuilt of steel, as was that on Belknap Mountain in the 1920s, and stairs and an observation platform were also added, primarily for the convenience of hikers who visited the summit. At one time, watchmen were stationed on these towers daily at the peak of the fire-danger season, but today, they are only manned sporadically at peak periods.

The Belknap Mountain tower, which was increased in height by ten feet in 1979, is today a popular hiking destination, and it is the tower's observation deck that gives those who make the hike up the mountain spectacular views of the lake and surrounding area. This tower is also interesting as it was very close to an aircraft crash in 1972. A Piper Archer aircraft departed the Laconia Airport on June 18, 1972, bound for Great Barrington, Massachusetts, with a flight instructor and student aboard when it disappeared altogether. The plane and the remains of its occupants were subsequently found nearly a year later about two-tenths of a mile below the summit, the aircraft having slammed into the side of Belknap Mountain and subsequently caught fire, which destroyed its locator. The remnants of that aircraft, including engine and wing components, are still there today and are a popular added hiking destination.

Another fire tower that is still remaining in the area is the Red Hill tower in Moultonborough. It can be accessed by turning onto Bean Road from Route 25 in Center Harbor, then taking a right onto Sibley Road and a left onto Red Hill Road, where a parking lot for trails to the summit can be found. This tower was built in 1927–28 and replaced a fire lookout that was located on Mount Israel in neighboring Sandwich. Though details are uncertain, photos show that the lookout facility on Mount Israel was a tripod open platform, not a tower, and that may have been a factor for the building of a more substantial tower on Red Hill. The summit was first named Red Mountain by historian Jeremy Belknap in 1791 and gets its name from the redness of its oak tree leaves in the fall season. The tower in Moultonborough came about because Center Harbor summer resident Ernest Dane, a Harvard graduate and Boston banker who owned much of the farmland in the area, offered to build a tower if the state would maintain the site. This agreement was accepted, and Dane contracted with the New Hampshire Structural Steel Company of Manchester to build a tower, complete with cab and phone lines, at a cost of $1,175. The structure was raised from a height of 27 feet to 37 feet in 1972 with an observation platform added and has operated almost continuously as a fire tower since its inception. In 1981, it was closed when the state decided to close most of its fire towers, but the

The Belknap Mountain fire tower still operates today as a lookout station but is only manned at peak or dangerous periods.

land reverted to its original owners and was subsequently leased to the town. The tower continued in operation under the authority of the Lakes Region Mutual Fire Aid Association. The man with the longest association with the Red Hill fire tower is Moultonborough fire warden Ed Maheux, who first manned the tower beginning in 1988 and did so for over twenty years. Among the dangers he has faced was a large fire that temporarily trapped him in the tower in 1989. Annual reports for the town of Moultonborough offer up some interesting statistics regarding Maheux's work at the tower. In the period running from April through October 2001, for example, the tower assisted 22 people, reported twenty-two "smokes," discovered ninety-nine "smokes" and encountered 4,121 visitors. Interestingly, the summit where this tower is located is one of the most famous of the early tourist destinations in the Lakes Region. It was in neighboring Center Harbor that New England literary giants like John Greenleaf Whittier, Samuel Adams Drake and Henry David Thoreau were visitors, with the latter climbing to the top of Red Hill long before the fire tower was built, in July 1858. Since 2000, the Lakes Region Conservation Trust has owned the summit property, leasing the tower to the Moultonborough Fire Department. To this day, Red Hill remains a popular destination among hikers, with thousands of people making the trek to the 2,029-foot summit every year.

Our third tower under consideration is the second oldest, by a few years, in the region, and the one that, for some reason, has been the subject of much misinformation. This is the Abenaki Tower in Tuftonboro, located on Route 109 heading west, just past Wawbeek Road, its entranceway highlighted by a stone tower sign. The tower got its start in 1923 when two Boston men were hiking on Edgerly Hill in Tuftonboro, "gazing out over clear pastures at the waters of Lake Winnipesaukee." Because of forest fires and timber cutting, the whole area was then clear, not wooded as it is today. In any event, the men suggested that it would be the perfect spot for a recreational tower to enhance visitors' views of the lake and "quickly organized a group of like-minded friends and neighbors" as the Abenaki Tower Association. The tower and association were so named because the site was said to be the location of several ancient Abenaki Indian trails. The land was purchased in February 1924 for $800 from John Edgerly, and a wooden tower was built on the site by Lewis McIntire of Tuftonboro for $500. His work was deemed "splendid." The tower was formally dedicated in July 1924 with a crowd of 125 people in attendance. It has always been free and open to the public and was a popular attraction for those staying at the nearby Wawbeek Resort Lodges for many years. While it has often been written that the Abenaki

The Abenaki Tower in Tuftonboro after its rebuilding in 1978. It offers excellent views of Lake Winnipesaukee.

Tower was built as a fire tower and was even used to spot German aircraft during World War II, none of these statements is true. By 1972, the tower had become somewhat decrepit and the renewed forest was obstructing its view, so action was needed, with the result that a newer and taller tower, designed by Tuftonboro builder Bill Cornell, was built in 1977–78 at a cost of $12,000 by Kirk Titus of Wolfeboro. Most of this cost was covered by private fundraising, with the exception of a small contribution from the town and a small grant from a private organization. Since that time, another round of tree clearing at the site has been performed to maintain the view—and what a view it offers! It is the easiest by far of all the local towers to reach and is well worth a visit. Interestingly, this tower, still maintained by the Abenaki Tower and Trail Association, remains a wooden structure to this day. Its renovation in 1978 used utility poles in the construction obtained from "power company supply sources."

CHAPTER 20

THE ONLY AIRPORT OF ITS KIND IN THE LOWER FORTY-EIGHT

I n Alton Bay, at the eastern end of Lake Winnipesaukee, you can find one of the most unusual historic sites around the lake. The youngest of the hidden history sites detailed in this book, it is not visible at all times of the year, and sometimes it can be invisible for a year or more at a time. So, what is this mysterious historic site? I am referring, as some who live in the region may suspect, to the Alton Bay ice runway, which is the only ice airfield of its kind in the lower forty-eight states that operates as a publicly licensed and FAA approved airport. Indeed, when it is open in the winter months, any small aircraft can land here free of charge, as long as they can get a grip on the idea of landing and taking off on the ice—no easy task even for the most experienced of pilots.

The Alton Bay ice runway had its beginnings in 1953, when Alton native Judson Downing (1920–2006), a lifelong resident of the town, applied and received approval for a seaplane base in Alton Bay. Not surprisingly, Downing, whose family was well known and respected in Alton from the beginning of the twentieth century, was a pilot who had served in the U.S. Army Air Corps during World War II and owned Downing's Landing at the end of the bay. After the war, he operated a business flying tourists over Lake Winnipesaukee in his Cessna aircraft on sightseeing tours but saw the seaplane base as yet another attraction to draw outside visitors, as well as to provide an official landing site for the seaplanes that operated on the lake in the summer months. So, that is how the Alton Bay Seaplane Base, FAA identification number B18, was born. It is perhaps not so surprising that

Downing established an airport here. He loved flying and adventure—his speedboat Legionnaire 75 was said to be the fastest public speedboat in the world for a time—and he loved his community. For a time, the seaplane base only operated in the summer months, but in the late 1960s or early 1970s, it was decided to apply for wintertime runway on the ice, and so the Alton Bay ice runway came into existence. Details about its early years of operation are scattered, but by the early 2000s, the ice runway seems to have faded away and was out of business entirely for about two years until it was revived in 2009 by local contractor and builder Paul La Rochelle, a member of the Alton Business Association. The group was originally looking for a place to hold helicopter rides when the idea of reviving the ice runway came to mind as a way to promote tourism in the winter off-season and support local restaurants and businesses. La Rochelle, with the help of Steve Bell, got things off the ground by getting in touch with the Bureau of Aeronautics at the New Hampshire Department of Transportation and worked with its aviation planner to get the necessary state approval. In addition to La Rochelle, six local volunteers who have been instrumental in operating and maintaining the ice runway over the years are Steve Bell, Bob Burton (who has served the longest), Rick Finethy, Roger Sample, Brian Mitchell and Nick Buonopane. Together, along with other occasional volunteers, these men have maintained the ice runway for over a decade. The ice runway itself is 3,000 feet long, about 170 feet wide and has a 50-foot taxiway. The south end of the runway has a parking ramp and an area that measures about 700 feet long by about 125 feet wide, which can accommodate some forty planes. Many of the planes that land here are of the single-engine type, some vintage in nature, manufactured by Cessna, Piper and Bonanza, though some twin-engine planes have landed here, as well as modern aircraft by Cirrus. However, through the years all sorts of other small craft have made their appearance here, including old biplanes, ultra-lights, helicopters and even a glider pulled by an old Piper Cub that has made many a yearly appearance.

The ice runway has been managed since 2009 by La Rochelle, as the state requires that someone be formally in charge, and certification papers are drawn up to that effect every year. While he receives a small stipend for his work, it does not even come close to matching all the work that La Rochelle does. But he is not concerned about this, because the ice runway, in effect, is a labor of love he performs for the community. He also makes it clear that he "can't do it without the volunteers." Interestingly, plans for the establishment of the ice runway are usually begun in late December by La Rochelle, with

An aerial view of the Alton Bay ice runway and parking area (*at left*). *Courtesy RandPeckPhoto.*

his phone "ringing off the hook" from about December 25 onward. It is at that time that he begins to make frequent, sometimes daily, checks on the ice in Alton Bay at various locations and meticulously documents his findings as to its thickness, as well as doing video posts. Indeed, it is not enough that the lake be frozen over; the ice has to have a consistent thickness of twelve inches or more in all locations, enough to safely support not just the aircraft but also the large snowplow trucks that groom the runway, before it can officially open. Proper ice thickness is the most critical aspect of the runway, and sometimes it never happens. In fact, the Alton ice runway as recently as 2019 never opened for the winter season because it was a mild winter and the ice on the bay never did reach the required thickness, a standard that was set by La Rochelle and has been accepted by the state for many years.

In those years when the ice does reach the correct thickness, that's where the real work begins. This consists of plowing the entire runway and taxiing and parking areas and getting the needed equipment set up. This includes the three portable radios provided by the state so that pilots can be communicated with, as well as a directional sock, many warning and safety signs and numerous yellow and orange cones used to mark the runway at intervals of about 150 to 200 feet. Once set up, the ice runway is inspected by state officials and, once approved, is an official airport and is treated as such. Hikers, skaters, ice fishermen and snowmobilers alike must stay out of the designated area, and La Rochelle and his crew have the authority to enforce restrictions, though, luckily, few disputes ever arise. As La Rochelle notes, "There's enough room out there on the ice for everyone to play." This is a distinct change from the 1980s and '90s, when battles between the earlier airport manager and locals on the ice were more pronounced. As with any official airport, there are rules and protocols that must be followed by La Rochelle (who is not a pilot) and incoming and outbound pilots alike. Though the airport is officially unmanned, with no control tower, pilots must still fly in legal patterns, and the radios are used to communicate with pilots regarding overall weather and wind conditions, the condition of the ice runway specifically and whether there is enough room to accommodate a landing. Other than this basic information, the airport manager in his communications has no authority to tell a pilot how to operate his aircraft or how to land and takeoff. On the busiest anticipated days of the season, usually Saturdays and Sundays, assistance often comes from the state capital, with a New Hampshire aviation official spending the day helping out.

Because landing on an ice runway is such an unusual and unique experience, pilots from all over New England and beyond make their appearance here. As La Rochelle notes, it is "a very safe operation. Pilots new to the experience are encouraged to fly in with someone who has already landed here," and all pilots are required by federal law to check the Notices to Airmen (NOTAMs) on the FAA website. Veteran commercial pilot Rand Peck, who grew up in nearby Tuftonboro and has made frequent visits here in his 1947 Piper Cub and 1946 Cessna 140, commented that "landing at

An aircraft's landing gear collapses after a tough landing on the Alton ice runway. *Courtesy RandPeckPhoto.*

Alton was always a challenge, mostly due to no braking....Landing on bare ice with a crosswind made it difficult to slow down straight ahead." He also commented, "Turning around at the end of the runway with no brakes and wind to taxi to the parking area was a challenge, as was maneuvering in that area." As for takeoffs, Peck commented, "You needed to think well ahead of your airplane. I saw a lot of 'go-arounds' as trailing airplanes in the pattern didn't think to give the guy in front of them additional time to clear the runway....Much to think about here."

While accidents have occurred here, they are rare and of the minor type. Only four incidents have taken place since 2009, three of these being aircraft that slid into a snowbank after landing. Other incidents, such as prop-strikes, flat tires and broken landing gear, have occurred, but these are to be expected. The most serious accident involved the landing of an experimental aircraft. The pilot panicked and the wing of the aircraft dipped low and caught a snowbank, causing it to flip over. Luckily, no major injuries occurred. However, like any airport, when even minor accidents happen, the runway is shut down, state and federal authorities have to be notified and the aircraft photographed and then moved and roped off for future investigation, but usually disruptions of this type are minor.

The response of the pilots who have made a landing at the Alton ice runway has been overwhelmingly favorable, it being a unique experience, and those pilots who arrive here for the first time even receive a state certificate for their unusual achievement. Indeed, many pilots would probably echo the comments of Rand Peck, who states, "It was fun flying and as close as I'll ever get to bush flying!" As to the public response, that has been equally favorable. Indeed, it is quite a sight to see these planes come in low over the bay to make their landing, and whether or not you're an aviation enthusiast, you can't help but be thrilled by the scene.

While the ice runway in a good year operates for anywhere from eight to ten weeks, the best time to see flight activity here is on a perfect winter weekend, when the skies are sunny, the winds are light and the temperature is hovering just around the freezing mark. On these days, as La Rochelle recalls, "it gets nuts...it's pretty crazy," with constant flight activity from the hours of 7:00 a.m. to 4:00 p.m., with the busiest time typically being from 9:00 a.m. to 2:00 p.m. (so plan ahead!). On days like this, it's all hands on deck for La Rochelle and his crew, with help from a state aviation specialist to keep things running smoothly at a time when as many as forty planes might be in the area, either waiting to land, on the taxiway or already landed and parked. One of the peak weekends is usually during the annual

Pilot Rand Peck's vintage Cessna on the ice at Alton Bay. Classic planes like this are a common sight on the runway. *Courtesy RandPeckPhoto*.

Winter Carnival in mid-February, but no matter what the weekend may be, when the planes are landing on the Alton ice runway, it's good for local businesses and restaurants, where pilots and their passengers can find a place to eat and do some local shopping during their sojourn. Of course, the ice runway is also open on weekdays, and some pilots prefer to fly in when conditions are less hectic.

So, for those who think of Lake Winnipesaukee in the wintertime as just a place for snowmobiling and ice-fishing, think again and come on down to Alton Bay in January or February on a nice weekend, and you may just get to experience one of the most unusual aspects of aviation history in New Hampshire. Of course, I hardly need to mention it, but if you're a pilot and you've never made the wintertime landing on the Alton ice runway, maybe it's time to make a new flight plan.

BIBLIOGRAPHY

Chapter 1

Belknap, Jeremy. *The History of New Hampshire*. Vol. 1. Dover, NH: Stevens, Ela, & Wadleigh, 1831.

Denormandie, Frank, and R. Stuart Wallace. "National Register of Historic Places Inventory—Nomination Form—Endicott Rock." Laconia, NH: 1975–76. npgallery.nps.gov/NRHP/GetAsset/NRHP/80000264_text.

Chapter 2

Mayo, Lawrence Shaw. *John Wentworth: Governor of New Hampshire 1767–1775*. Cambridge, MA: Harvard University Press, 1921.

Parker, Benjamin Franklin. *History of the Town of Wolfeborough New Hampshire*. Wolfeborough, NH, 1901.

Starbuck, David. "America's Oldest Summer Place." *Archaeology* 41, no. 6 (November–December 1988): 60–61.

Chapter 3

Knoblock, Glenn A. *Cemeteries Around Lake Winnipesaukee*. Charleston, SC: Arcadia Publishing, 2006.

————. *Historic Meetinghouses and Churches of New Hampshire*. Charleston, SC: Arcadia Publishing, 2019.

Wiley, Frederick L. *Life and Influences of the Rev. Benjamin Randall: Founder of the Free Baptist Denomination*. Philadelphia: American Baptist Publication Society, 1915.

Chapter 4

Hanaford, Mary Elisabeth Neal. *Family Records of Branches of the Hanaford, Thompson, Huckins, Prescott, Smith, Neal, Haley, Lock, Swift, Plumer, Leavitt, Wilson, Green, and Allied Families*. Rockford, IL, 1915.

Heald, Bruce D. *New Hampshire Learnin Days: Dudley Leavitt, "Master": An Historic Review*. Meredith, NH: Heald Enterprises, 1987.

Leavitt, Dudley. *Leavitt's Farmer's Almanac and Miscellaneous Year Book, 1851*. Franklin, NH: Peabody & Daniel, 1850.

Prescott, Polly A. "Some Memories of Dudley Leavitt." *Granite Monthly* 20, no. 1 (1896): 265.

Chapter 5

Dionne, Mark. "Paths to New Hampshire's Native Past." *New Hampshire Magazine*, June 13, 2017. www.nhmagazine.com/paths-to-new-hampshires-native-past.

Haley, John W. *Tuftonboro, New Hampshire: An Historical Sketch*. Concord, NH: Rumford Press, 1923.

Knoblock, Glenn A. *Cemeteries Around Lake Winnipesaukee*. Charleston, SC: Arcadia Publishing, 2006.

Whittier, John Greenleaf. *The Collected Works of John Greenleaf Whittier*. Vol. 4. Cambridge, MA: Riverside Press, 1894.

Chapter 6

Candee, Richard M. "National Register of Historic Places Inventory— Nomination Form—Belknap-Sulloway Mill." Laconia, NH, 1970. npgallery.nps.gov/NRHP/GetAsset/NRHP/71000046_text.

————. "National Register of Historic Places Inventory—Nomination Form—Busiel-Seeburg Mill." Laconia, NH, 1971. npgallery.nps.gov/NRHP/GetAsset/NRHP/71000047_text.

Hurd, D. Hamilton, ed. *History of Merrimack and Belknap Counties, New Hampshire*. Philadelphia: J.W. Lewis, 1885.

Parker, Benjamin Franklin. *History of the Town of Wolfeborough, New Hampshire*. Wolfeborough, NH, 1901.

Peters, Esther. *History of the Belknap Mill*. Laconia: New Hampshire Vocational Technical College, 1987. www.belknapmill.org/Mill_History_by_Esther_Peters.pdf.

Chapter 7

"The Alton Monthly Meeting or Church Records." Alton, NH, handwritten manuscript, 1803–1842, 9, 96, 98–100, 104–10, 118, 128, 146.

Knoblock, Glenn A. *Cemeteries Around Lake Winnipesaukee*. Charleston, SC: Arcadia Publishing, 2006.

———. *Historic Meetinghouses and Churches of New Hampshire*. Charleston, SC: Arcadia Publishing, 2019.

Chapter 8

Bliss, Sylvester. *Memoirs of William Miller*. Boston: Joshua V. Himes, 1858.

Hurd, D. Hamilton, ed. *History of Merrimack and Belknap Counties, New Hampshire*. Philadelphia: J.W. Lewis, 1885.

Chapter 9

Aldredge, James. "A Railroad Man Started the Harvard and Yale Regatta." *The Boston and Maine Railroad Employees Magazine* 18, no. 7 (July 1946): 8–9.

Harvard University. "Harvard Aquatics: A Retrospect of Thirty Years." February 9, 1887. www.thecrimson.com/article/1887/2/9/harvard-aquatics-boating-at-harvard-has.

Mendenhall, Thomas C. *The Harvard-Yale Boat Race 1852–1924 and the Coming of Sport to the American College*. Mystic, CT: Mystic Seaport, 1993.

Pucin, Diane. "A Row Involving Tradition's Start." *Los Angeles Times*, November 30, 2006. www.latimes.com/archives/la-xpm-2006-nov-30-sp-oars30-story.html.

Smith, Ronald Austin. *Pay for Play: A History of Big-Time College Athletic Reform*. Urbana: University of Illinois Press, 2011.

———. *Sports and Freedom: The Rise of Big-Time College Athletics*. New York: Oxford University Press, 1988.

Chapter 10

Bartlett, Asa W. *History of the Twelfth Regiment, New Hampshire Volunteers in the War of the Rebellion*. Concord, NH: I.C. Evans, 1897.

Fox, William F. *Regimental Losses in the American Civil War, 1861–1865*. Albany, NY: Albany Publishing Co., 1889.

Hurd, D. Hamilton, ed. *History of Merrimack and Belknap Counties, New Hampshire*. Philadelphia: J.W. Lewis, 1885.

Chapter 11

Ayling, Augustus D. *Revised Register of the Soldiers and Sailors of New Hampshire in the War of the Rebellion 1861–1866*. Concord, NH: Ira C. Evans, 1895.

Pettengill, M.J. "A Partial List of Those Buried at the Carroll County Farm Cemetery, Ossipee, New Hampshire." www.mjpettengill.com/the-paupers. Readers should note that research on this cemetery is ongoing and that Pettengill has revised this list as new information has come to light. While there are some minor errors in the listing, it is an excellent resource.

Chapter 12

Heard, Patricia L. "Isaac Adams: Inventive Genius (1802–1883)." *Seventy-Fourth Annual Excursion of the Sandwich Historical Society*, August 22, 1993, Sandwich, NH, 11–22.

Porter, Boone (Sandwich Historical Society). "Niobe and the Great Wall of Sandwich." www.sandwichhistorical.org/niobe.html.

Rogers, S.A. "Stories from Sandwich, New Hampshire: A Living Showcase of Eastern White Pine." June 30, 2018. easternwhitepine.org/stories-from-sandwich-new-hampshire-a-living-showcase-of-eastern-white-pine.

Chapter 13

Clarke, Warren E. "An Invisible Presence: African Americans in a Rural New Hampshire Town." 2014. www.gilmantonnhhistory.org/ckfinder/userfiles/files/Demographics/2014AfricanAmericans.pdf.

Hanaford, Mary Elizabeth Neal. *Meredith, New Hampshire: Annals and Genealogies*. Concord, NH: Rumford Press, 1932.

Jennings, Ellen C. *The History of New Durham: From the First Settlement to the Present*. Manchester, NH: Fitzpatrick Printers, 1962.

Knoblock, Glenn A. *African American Historic Burial Grounds and Gravesites of New England*. Jefferson, NC: McFarland & Co., 2016.

———. *Strong and Brave Fellows: New Hampshire's Black Soldiers and Sailors in the American Revolution, 1775–1784*. Jefferson, NC: McFarland & Co., 2003.

Lancaster, Daniel. *The History of Gilmanton*. Gilmanton, NH: Alfred Prescott, 1845.

State of Massachusetts, Adjutant General's Office. *Massachusetts Soldiers, Sailors, and Marines in the Civil War*. Vol 6. Norwood, MA: Norwood Press, 1937.

Chapter 14

Ayling, Augustus D. *Revised Register of the Soldiers and Sailors of New Hampshire in the War of the Rebellion, 1861–1866*. Concord, NH: Ira C. Evans, 1895.

New Hampshire Veterans Association. *New Hampshire Veterans Association Fortieth Encampment 1875–1916 Official Programme*. Laconia, NH, 1916.

Chapter 15

Heald, Bruce D. *Follow the Mount (An Historical Review)*. Meredith, NH: Winnipesaukee Flagship Corp., 1991.

Stanton, Samuel Ward. *Stanton's American Steam Vessels*. Mineola, NY: Dover Publications, 2002.

Chapter 16

Ehrensperger, Harold. *The Fire Between the Fires: A Brief History of Gilmanton, New Hampshire Academy*. Gilmanton, NH: Gilmanton Historical Society, April 1973.

Lancaster, Daniel. *The History of Gilmanton*. Gilmanton, NH: Alfred Prescott, 1845.

Ruell, David L. "National Register of Historic Places Nomination Form—Gilmanton Academy." Meredith, NH, Lakes Region Planning Commission, March 12, 1983. npgallery.nps.gov/NRHP/GetAsset/NRHP/83001127_text.

Chapter 17

Hays, Warren H. "The Cocheco Railroad." *The Boston & Maine Bulletin* 4, no. 6 (Summer 1977). Lowell, MA, Boston & Maine Railroad Historical Society.

Libby, R.C. *Rails to Wolfeborough*. Wolfeboro, NH: Wolfeboro Rail Road, 1984.

New Hampshire, State of. *Forty-Third Annual Report of the Railroad Commissioner of the State of New Hampshire*. Manchester, NH: John B. Clarke, Printer, 1887.

Chapter 18

Green, Rick. "Unmarked Graves a Possibility at State School Site." *Laconia Daily Sun*, December 20, 2018. www.laconiadailysun.com/news/local/unmarked-graves-a-possibility-at-state-school-site/article_9217db1c-ede0-11e8-b4f1-77839ffe8aee.html.

Krumm, Janet M. "The History of Laconia State School." *New Hampshire Challenge* 16, no. 4 (Summer 2004).

Lost in Laconia. Directed by Bil Rogers, written by Gordon Dubois, Bil Rogers and Janet Krumm. 1L Media, 2010.

Chapter 19

Abenaki Tower and Trail Association. "About the Abenaki Tower." abenakitower.org/about-the-abenaki-tower-trail-association.

Baird, Iris W., and Chris Haartz. *A Field Guide to New Hampshire Fire Towers*. Concord: New Hampshire Department of Resources and Economic Development, Forests and Lands, 2005.

Moultonborough, Town of. *Annual Report of the Town of Moultonborough, New Hampshire*. Meredith, NH: News Office, 2002.

Rice, Jane. "History of Red Hill." kanasatka.org/history-of-red-hill.

Chapter 20

Most of the information on the operations of the Alton ice runway is derived from my telephone interview with airport manager Paul La Rochelle conducted on November 15, 2020, while a pilot's point of view has been provided by Rand Peck in email communications with the author.

ABOUT THE AUTHOR

Historian Glenn A. Knoblock is the author of *The American Clipper Ship* and eight books with Arcadia and The History Press, including *New Hampshire Covered Bridges*, *Brewing in New Hampshire* (with James Gunter), *Cemeteries Around Lake Winnipesaukee* and *Historic Burial Grounds of the New Hampshire Seacoast*. He resides in Wolfeboro Falls, New Hampshire.